STORIES WITHOUT ENDINGS

SNAPSHOTS

GLOBE FEARON EDUCATIONAL PUBLISHER
A Division of Simon & Schuster
Upper Saddle River, New Jersey

Project Editor: Lynn W. Kloss
Editorial Assistant: Kristen Shepos
Editorial Supervisor: Steven Otfinoski, Sandra Widener
Story Writers: Dina Anastasio, Arvin W. Casas,
   Janice L. Greene, Joyce Haines, Kinerette Hasson,
   Krista L. Kanenwisher, Lottie E. Porch,
   Brenda Lane Richardson, Kristen Shepos, Sandra Widener
Production Manager: Penny Gibson
Production Editor: Linda Greenberg
Marketing Manager: Sandra Hutchison
Interior Electronic Design and Art Supervision: Joan Jacobus
Illustrator: Ted Enik
Electronic Page Production: Ewing Systems
Cover Design: Patricia Smythe
Cover Illustration: © Jerry McDaniel '94

Printed in the United States of America.
5 6 7 8 9 10 05 04 03 02 01 00

ISBN: 0-835-91212-4

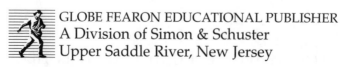

GLOBE FEARON EDUCATIONAL PUBLISHER
A Division of Simon & Schuster
Upper Saddle River, New Jersey

Contents

About This Book   vii

1. Friendship   1

Tears, laughter, problems, and triumphs—
the characters in these stories face the
same joys and agonies as you do. As you
read these stories, think about your own
experiences. How should *you treat a friend?*

The Election   1
Whose Band Is It?   3
The Trouble with Mr. Jones   5
The Accident   7
Doing Tutor Time   9
A Friend in Need   11
My Turn   13
Jimmy's Choice   15

2. Heart to Heart   19

Love can be heartbreaking, fun, and even
downright scary. Read these stories and try
to decide—what would you *do for love?*

A Girl's Best Friend   19
Daydreamer   21
Surprise Attack   23
The Photo   24
Letter Across Time   26

3. Peer Pressure   30

*If you've ever felt you had to do something
because a friend asked you to do it, you'll
appreciate these stories. Staying loyal to a
friend is everything—or is it?*

Almost Perfect   30
Losing It All   32
Hold-up   34
New Shoes   36
The Ride   38
The Book   40

4. Moral Choices   44

*You make more moral choices than you
think. The characters in these stories are
dealing with questions of morality—but
what they do about them is up to you.*

Loyalties   44
The Choice   46
Rush Hour   48
The Invitation   50
One Day Long Ago   51
The Secret   53
The Third Street Beggar   54
Playing with Fire   56

5. Taking Risks   60

*In this unit, people are facing some big
problems. Should she meet a mysterious
stranger? Should he risk everything on making a perfect foul shot? Read on; then decide.*

The Watcher   60
Foul Shots   62
A Long Way Down   63
Elisha's Dog   66
Just My Luck   67
On the Road   68

6. Breaking with Tradition 72

How do you choose between loyalty to your family and loyalty to yourself? Breaking away or sticking with tradition—that's the choice these characters have to make.

In Line with Sandy Koufax 72
Big Mama's Letter 73
Promised Land 75
Warrior Week 77
Music Lesson 80

7. Turning Point 84

How do you deal with problems? Life is full of turning points that help you decide who you are and what you stand for. You can decide how these characters should deal with their dilemmas.

The Boy in the Mall 84
Helping Hand 85
Team Spirit 87
Managing 89
Parents, Please Come Home 91
A Different Face 93
Big Money 95
Treasure 97
Doing Time 99

8. In the Danger Zone 103

How would you react if you had to make a life-or-death decision? In these stories, you have the chance to decide what you'd do if you faced real danger.

White Water 103
The Prisoner and the Proof 105
The *Titanic* Is Sinking! 107
The People Next Door 109
The Test of Fire 111
The Danger Outside 113

9. Family Ties

Annoying younger brothers, impossible demands by parents—they shape our lives. As you read these stories, think about how you deal with the people you live with every day—and what advice you'd offer to the people in these stories.

9. Family Ties 117

'Tis the Gift to Be Simple 117
Robbery in Progress 119
Bread 121
Many Happy Returns 123
The Hat 125

10. Other Worlds

Let your imagination wander to planets far from home, to exotic worlds where nothing is what you expect. Tread carefully because you'll have to find a way out of some unusual situations.

10. Other Worlds 129

In the Colony of Saurnia 129
Kavlon V 131
How Do You Say "Friend"? 133

About This Book

This book can be an adventure. Within its pages are people who must decide whether to join gangs. Other people must decide whether to betray a friend, take a chance on love, or even risk their lives.

The best part, though, is the ending that you write. In most of the stories you have read, the author decides what happens. This book is quite different. In these stories, you decide who wins and who loses, whether the characters will do the right thing or take the easy way out. It's in your hands.

As you read these stories, think about how you might handle the situations. Think about what others you know might do if faced with each problem. Use your own experience to find answers. You might also consider a completely new solution. Sometimes, those are better than the obvious ones. You can use your imagination to think up the perfect, unexpected ending.

As you think about the ending you'll write, though, remember that you're writing for characters in a story, not for yourself. Try to make the decision you think the *character* might make. Characters have their own lives and ideas. What they would do might be quite different from the choice you would make.

Some of these characters may face unpleasant situations you recognize. If the plot of one story makes you uncomfortable, you might want to finish another one instead. It is possible, though, that thinking about the situation the character faces may be a good way for you to think about your own experience. Thinking about the story may provide you with some new ways of dealing with your difficulties.

You can also find suggestions for ways to finish these stories by talking over the situations with friends, parents, or brothers and sisters. Play the scene out in your mind and "see" what might happen next. You could try different endings to see which one works best. Also think about checking how differently your friends ended the stories. You might get together with a friend and read the story aloud, trying out different endings.

Above all, have fun. Relax and let your imagination take over. You might surprise yourself with the answers you find.

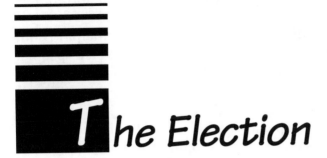

*T*he Election

"So you'll do it, right?"

Nicole was waiting for Yvonne to answer.

"Yeah, I'll be your campaign manager," Yvonne said without enthusiasm.

"Great," Nicole said, grinning. "You know, if I win the election for student council vice-president, I'll get to sit in a meeting with Tony Salvatore every week."

"Uh-huh," Yvonne answered absentmindedly. "So what's your election platform?" she asked.

Nicole looked at her strangely. "My what?"

"Your platform." Yvonne sighed. "What issues are you going to talk about for the election?" She was already sorry she had agreed to be Nicole's campaign manger, but she had made the commitment.

"Hmm." Nicole shut her eyes and thought. Suddenly, she snapped her fingers and smiled. "My platform is—if I win the election for student council vice-president, I will get rid of the dress code."

"Wow! You'd definitely win if you promised that," Yvonne replied. Everyone hated the dress code—no hats, no brand-name sneakers, and no baggy jeans. But Yvonne knew that the administration wasn't budging. There was no way Nicole could keep her promise.

"What about starting a schoolwide community service day?" Yvonne suggested.

"Bo-ring!" Nicole sang. "We'll stick with my idea. I'll meet you after school to start making posters. See ya!" She grabbed her things and left. Yvonne sat for a moment and thought about the mess she had gotten herself into.

"Yvonne!" She looked up to find Vice-Principal Diehl smiling at her. Ms. Diehl was one of her favorite people.

"What's up?" Ms. Diehl asked. "You look like you're thinking hard."

"Sort of," Yvonne replied. "I guess I'm just busy."

"I wanted to speak to you," Ms. Diehl said. "I was speaking with some teachers about the student council elections, and your name came up."

Yvonne's eyes widened. "It did?" she asked.

"A number of teachers feel you'd make an excellent vice-president. Have you thought about running?"

Yvonne was so surprised that she could barely speak. "Uh, I, uh, no, not really," she stammered.

"Well, I think you're perfect for the job. Of course, the decision is up to you."

"Thanks, Ms. Diehl. I'll think about it."

The vice-principal smiled warmly. "Come talk to me if you have any questions." She waved goodbye and walked toward her office.

Yvonne couldn't believe it. The vice-principal thought she was perfect for the job!

Yvonne began to think about how her speech to the school would sound. Dozens of ideas started to swirl around in her head.

Then she suddenly remembered her promise to Nicole. How could she back out and then run against her?

But I'm coming up with ideas that can actually work, Yvonne thought. Nicole's just running because she wants Tony Salvatore to notice her.

Yvonne could barely pay attention in her afternoon classes. Was it fair to back out on Nicole? Or was it worse to help someone she knew wasn't right for the job? Finally, her last class of the day was over.

Nicole caught up with Yvonne on her way out the front door. "Hey, ready to help me become the next vice-president?" Nicole asked.

Yvonne took a deep breath and replied . . .

Whose Band Is It?

Olivia strolled to the front of the stage and introduced the band. "Ladies and gentlemen," she said. "Meet Strange But True. We have Sonya on drums, Greta on keyboard, and Janet on bass. I'm Olivia, and I play lead guitar."

As Olivia introduced them, the members of Strange But True nodded. Then they began to play. Olivia, who was also lead vocalist, stood in front as usual. She sang her favorite song, the same one she always sang first, and it was loud.

"It'll get them moving," she always said. "We want them jumping around on their feet, and that's the song to do it."

But tonight they weren't on their feet. They were sitting at their tables, and they didn't care about the band.

"We need a new opener," Sonya suggested after the gig. "We aren't getting to them, and they aren't interested."

"I'll think about it, but now I have to go," Olivia said. "We'll talk about it tomorrow."

When she was gone, the rest of the band sat at a table and looked at one another.

"We aren't making it, guys. Something's very wrong," Janet said.

"We all know what it is," Greta reminded them.

The band sat in silence for a very, very long time. Every one of them understood exactly what was wrong with the band, but no one had the nerve to say it out loud.

The club manager joined them a few minutes later. He pulled out his checkbook, handed them a check, and said, "I'm afraid I won't be needing you again."

When he saw the desperate looks on their faces, he pulled out a chair and sat down.

"Look," he explained, "I like all four of you, but I have a business to run here. Let me give you some advice."

"You don't have to tell us," Sonya said.

"Then I don't understand what's happening with you, especially if you know why you're doing badly. Or maybe I do understand. Whose band is this, anyway?"

"Olivia started it," Sonya said. "It was her idea, her name, her band, her everything."

The man shrugged and responded, "Then you have a big problem, don't you?"

Sonya, Janet, and Greta held a meeting two nights later. They gathered in Sonya's basement to discuss the problem: Olivia.

"Look," Janet said. "This band is doomed if we don't do something fast."

"Like fire her?" Greta suggested.

"Yes," Janet agreed, "like fire her."

"We can't do that," Sonya said. "Olivia started this band. It was her idea, and she brought us all together."

"She's our good friend, and she'd do anything for us," Greta reminded them.

"Well, it'll be nobody's band if we don't get rid of her," Janet said. "Olivia is a terrible singer and she's a lousy guitar player. Just because she thinks she's great doesn't mean she is."

They looked at one another and sighed. That, of course, was the problem. Olivia was terrible, but she thought she was wonderful.

"So what can we do?" Sonya asked.

No one had an answer. They had to make a decision, and they had to do it quickly. So they did. The three of them decided to . . .

The Trouble with Mr. Jones

"He did it again, Josephine. He did it again," Felicia Whispering Dove *sobbed as she fell across her bed in the dorm room she shared with Josephine Thunderhawk.* They had become best friends ever since they met at the College of Inter-Tribal Nations two years ago. Felicia was Hopi. Josephine was Lakota. Even though they were as different as night and day, the young women respected and learned from one another.

Josephine was able to solve any calculus problem. Felicia had a gift for biology. On their reservations, they had both seen that those with an education had the best chance of escaping poverty. Both were determined to get the education they needed. But now a problem was threatening Felicia's hopes.

"Jones did it again," Felicia repeated, "right in front of the whole class. While he waited for me to recite the names of the northern nations, he sat there tapping his feet and looking out the window. I was really terrified. I couldn't even open my mouth. I almost died."

Richard Jones had taught the History of Native Cultures for seven years at the college. The only thing Felicia knew about him was that for some reason, he was constantly picking on her. He either ignored her or made cutting remarks about her during class. As a result, Felicia was terrified of him. She was terrified that she would fail his class, which was required. She also wondered if there were another reason for his behavior toward her. Did he hate her or was he just trying to push her to do her best?

"He's gone too far, Felicia, and you know he's not going to change," Josephine said angrily. "I've heard that he's done this to other girls, too. You have to confront him!"

"What if he laughs at me? Or tells me to get out? What do I do then? What if confronting him makes him so angry he picks on me even more? Maybe I could just try to work harder. . . . " Felicia said, her voice trailing off.

"You've got to do something, and you've got to do it now. Right now. You know you're smart. You know it," Josephine said. "If you showed a little guts, he might stop."

Felicia shook her head, miserably. "I don't know. I just don't know."

The next day in class, Mr. Jones was even ruder. "Felicia, see me after class," he said after she stammered her answer to a question in class.

"Come in," Mr. Jones said to Felicia after she knocked on his office door. He was sitting at his desk.

"Felicia," he said, "I'm not sure you're cut out for this class—or this college. I don't like to see you embarrassed every day, and that's what's happening. If you want to find another place to continue your education—a trade school, maybe—I'd be glad to help. What do you think?"

Felicia didn't know what to think. Was he just testing her? Or did he really believe what he was telling her?

"Mr. Jones," Felicia said, "I . . .

The Accident

Greg had great plans for that Saturday, and they all depended on Willie's truck.

Willie was at his apartment, watching the football game. "Sure," he said when Greg asked him if he could borrow the truck. "I'm not going anywhere till the game ends. Just have it back in a couple of hours, OK?"

"Sure," Greg responded. "Thanks!"

Greg drove down Harbor Way. The radio was blasting, and he felt good. He was headed to Big City Builders, where there was a lumber sale. He was going to build some shelves for his girlfriend Carol as a birthday present.

He was thinking about the wood he would buy when a woman stepped off the curb right in front of the truck.

He hit the horn—no sound came out!

He slammed on the brakes. There was a soft thump. The sound made his heart stop. He'd hit her!

He flew out of the truck. The woman was lying on the street, holding her leg. Her face was very pale.

He bent over her. "I'm sorry, lady, I . . ." His voice was shaking. He didn't know what to say.

A man had pulled up to the curb and was yelling into his car phone " . . . on Harbor Way at First. A woman has been injured. She was on foot, and this kid in a truck ran into her!" Greg shut his eyes. He felt sick.

The football game had been over for a long time when Greg finally made it back to Willie's apartment.

"What happened?" Willie demanded. "I've been stuck here all afternoon waiting for you!"

Greg said, "I had an accident. This woman was hit—because your horn didn't work! You didn't even tell me!"

"What is this?" Willie asked. "What do you mean, she was hit because the horn didn't work? You hit her?"

"I used the horn, and it didn't work," Greg answered. "She was stepping off the curb. There wasn't time to stop. She's got a broken leg, and she's going to sue!"

"That's too bad," Willie said slowly.

"Yeah? Well, it isn't all my fault," Greg said. "You have a truck that's dangerous because it doesn't have a working horn, and you didn't let me know about it!"

Willie's face was red now. "That horn didn't hit her, Buddy—you did! That accident happened because of the way you were driving!"

"It happened because you don't take care of your truck!" Greg yelled.

"Tell that to the judge!" Willie shouted.

Greg sat stiffly in the heavy wooden courtroom chair. Judge Sharilee Wilson had heard his story and then Willie's. It was time for her to decide. She finished reading notes she had made. She looked at Willie and then at Greg. Her face was perfectly blank. She said . . .

Doing Tutor Time

I have to do this stupid journal as part of my sentence. That's what they called it. It's part of my sentence—as if I were a criminal or something just for writing on the stupid walls. I don't care who reads this, either. It's stupid. They told me I have to write about tutoring this kid. Like what am I supposed to write? "David couldn't read today, either." Six months of writing in this journal and two whole months of tutoring, every single day? Anyone would think I had trashed the whole school.

So far, I've been tutoring this kid David for a week. So here goes: David still can't read.

The more I know about this kid, the sorrier I feel for him. He's been in about ten schools since he was a first grader. How can you make any friends doing that? How can you learn anything? I guess that's why he still can't read. Lot of good this is doing.

David comes in today, his eyes all red as if he's been crying. I ask him what's wrong. It turns out the kids in his class have been making fun of him because he stutters and can't read. Kids can be so crummy. So we sit down to work, and for the first time, I feel like something's happening. He's really trying. Maybe those kids did him a favor.

David came in today and gave me this smile like I was a hero or something. Then he gave me a hug. I could tell he was embarrassed by it, but I also could tell he wanted me to tell him it was OK. So I did. Then he told me about how his mother was gone all night again, and he got scared because he heard these noises. I asked him if his mom was gone a lot. He said yes, and I told him she was probably busy or something. Inside, though, I was mad. Why do people have kids if they're not going to take care of them?

Two more weeks and I'm finished. At least David's gotten something out of it. He's really reading better— but I would, too, if I had some kid spending an hour a day with me. An hour a day! When I think of what I could be doing with this time!

This is my last week with David. He asks me every day how many more days we have. I'm starting to feel like a real creep, but I want my life back. Someone else can teach him to read. Why should I? Why do I have to do this? Let his mother take a turn.

Yesterday, David came in, crying about how he's never going to see me again. I told him to cut it out. I told him it's basketball season now, and if I don't go to practice, I can't be on the team. That didn't seem to help. Nothing did. I told him I'd see him in school and stuff. He just cried harder. He grabbed on to my leg as if he were 3 years old or something. I didn't know what to do, and I got mad at him. I felt terrible, but I was tired of feeling like I was this kid's mother or something. I looked at that face of his, and his runny nose, and I made up my mind. I told him . . .

A Friend in Need

The little girl dropped the candy bar on the counter.

"How much?" she asked Lilly, as she held out her hand and showed Lilly her change.

Lilly took some coins. It was a slow night, so slow that Lilly was able to study. She tried to do her homework, but she couldn't think because she was too upset. Mr. Kirk had hollered at her again, and she was still shaking.

"Late again?" he had shouted. "How am I supposed to run a store when you wander in here late three times a week?"

"I had to help my mother because the baby's sick again," Lilly had explained.

"Is that my problem?" Mr. Kirk had screamed. "No! It is not my problem, and you only have one more chance, young lady, so watch your step!"

Lilly couldn't stop thinking about what he had said. She needed the job. Her family couldn't survive without her salary.

Lilly stared at her book and tried to concentrate. She had a quiz the next day, and maybe if she did well in school, she wouldn't have to work in a store forever. The words in the book spun around in her head. She needed sleep badly, but maybe she could sleep late this weekend.

Suddenly, the door crashed open, and her best friend Amy rushed in and threw herself on the counter.

"I am so glad you're here!" she whispered.

"What's up?" Lilly asked.

Amy couldn't speak because her breath was coming in quick jerks.

"I need your help," she gasped after a moment.

Lilly closed her book and waited for her friend to finish. "It's my grandmother, Lilly," Amy said. "She's sick with a high fever. I called the doctor, and he said she needs medicine right away. But I don't have any money."

Lilly knew that Amy was telling the truth because Amy's family had less money than her own.

Amy's eyes filled with tears. "I have to do something fast, Lilly, or I'm afraid she'll die."

Lilly hurried into the back room and fumbled through her coat pockets, but she could only find 50 cents. Fifty cents wouldn't buy much medicine.

"What about your mother?" she asked Amy.

Amy shook her head furiously. "She's away for the weekend, and I can't get in touch with her. I don't know who else to ask, Lil."

Lilly sat and watched the tears roll down Amy's face. She turned to the cash register, pushed a button, and moved back as the drawer opened.

Amy stared at the money and whispered, "I didn't mean for you to steal it."

"I know you didn't."

"You can't, Lilly!" Amy whispered. "You'll get in big trouble."

Lilly slammed the drawer and stared at her fingers. She realized that Amy was right. If she took any money, Mr. Kirk would know, and she would probably be fired.

"Maybe he won't know," Lilly said. "Maybe we can replace it before he finds out."

"But if we can't, you'll lose your job."

Lilly looked at her friend and sighed. Then she . . .

My Turn

Lucille sat alone in the back of the theater and watched the play, just as she did every day.

I'll never, ever, be a star, and I'll never go to Hollywood, she thought. I'll be stuck here forever.

A week ago, she thought she had made it. She thought she had the leading part in the school play. She knew she could do it, but they had chosen her best friend instead. Now Patty was the star, and Lucille was the understudy.

Jason came over and sat beside her. "There's a talent scout coming from the city tomorrow night," he said.

Lucille stared at him. "How do you know?" she asked.

"A couple of the kids were talking," he said.

Lucille didn't believe it, but what if it were true? Patty was good, but Lucille knew she was better. This was her chance to be noticed. But the only person the agent would see was Patty.

Lucille walked home very, very slowly. She felt sick. Lucille wanted to be a star more than anything. She had been dreaming about it all her life, and even though she knew that she should be happy for Patty, she wasn't.

Maybe she'll get sick, she thought.

She knew she should feel bad for thinking something like that, but she didn't.

Patty called at 8:00 that night when Lucille was doing her homework.

"You all right?" Patty asked.

"Sure. Why?" Lucille said.

"Well, I heard an agent's coming," Patty explained. "Did you hear that?"

"I heard it," Lucille sighed. "I'll bet you're glad."

Patty didn't say anything for a while, and then she

mumbled something that Lucille couldn't understand.

"What did you say?" Lucille asked.

"I said, 'Please don't be mad, because I can't help it.'"

Suddenly, Lucille felt awful. Patty was being so nice.

"I really like being your friend, and it's very important to me," Patty told her gently.

"I like being your friend, too," Lucille replied, and it was true. She did like being Patty's friend because Patty would do anything for her, and she was always kind. Lucille didn't want Patty to get sick, but she did wish that she could somehow take over Patty's role.

"Good luck tomorrow night," Lucille said.

Lucille called Patty at 4:00 the next day because she wanted to wish her good luck again. She wanted to tell her that she would always be her friend, but Patty was crying when she answered the phone.

"What's wrong?" Lucille asked.

"It's my baby sister," Patty explained. "She's really sick, Lucille, and Mom's afraid to leave her with a baby-sitter. She can't stay home from work tonight. She'll lose her job if she does."

"What about your grandmother?"

"She's in Philadelphia," Patty explained. "There's no one else, so Mom says that I have to stay home with her."

Lucille's heart jumped. Did this mean that she was going to be the star of the show after all?

Lucille knew that she should offer to take care of the baby, but she wanted that part more than anything in the world. She thought for a long time. Then she said . . .

Jimmy's Choice

Jimmy picked up the phone and punched in Cory's number. "You aren't going to believe this one," he said when Cory answered.

"Well, come on, Jimmy, hurry and tell me," Cory pleaded.

"I got the job."

Cory screamed. Jimmy had been working in that factory part-time for two years. First it was Saturdays, then it was after school, too, and now it was full-time.

"Let's meet at our special place at 6:00, and we'll celebrate," Cory suggested.

Cory and Jimmy had been best friends since they were 6. They had shared every important moment in their lives.

Cory was sitting on a tree stump when he arrived. She was watching the river roll gently by.

"This is my favorite place in the whole world," she told Jimmy. "I saw my first beaver in this river, and remember the time we saw that otter? I love this river more than anything."

"I know you do," Jimmy said.

Jimmy went over and sat beside her. "Wait'll I tell you about my job," he said. "It's amazing. I supervise five people and make sure that they fit all the pieces of the tires together right. They all like me, too."

"Sure they do," Cory said. She stood up and walked to the riverbank, leaned down, and ran her fingers through the water. Suddenly, her fingers touched something clammy. She grabbed it and held it up.

"What's that?" Jimmy called.

"It's a dead fish, and there's another one over there. I wonder if something's killing them."

Jimmy moved closer to the water and looked down.

The water looked clear and clean, but there were several dead fish floating near the riverbank.

"I'm going to find out what's killing these fish, and I'm going to get whoever is responsible!" Cory exclaimed.

For the next few days, Jimmy was so busy at work that he didn't have time to call Cory. When he finally did call her, she wouldn't speak to him, so he called her back again.

"Talk to me, Cory," he pleaded. "What did I do?"

"It's not what you did, it's where you work," Cory explained angrily. "I found out what's killing those fish, Jimmy, and it's your tire company. They're dumping junk into our river."

Jimmy couldn't think of anything to say. He loved the river, too, but not as much as Cory did.

"What can I do?" Jimmy asked.

"Why don't you try to make them stop?" Cory asked.

"You know I can't do that," Jimmy replied.

"Then quit, Jimmy," she insisted.

Jimmy didn't say anything for a long time. "But I love this job, Cory," he said at last.

"What's more important—your job, or our river?"

Jimmy thought about this. Then he said, "Cory . . .

IIII Thinking About the Stories

What do you mean when you say that someone is your friend? Do you mean that you and your friend share all of the same ideas and interests? Do you mean that you never disagree about anything? Most people—even best friends—disagree on at least a few issues. They usually work out their differences by talking to each other or by having someone help them work things out.

All of the stories in this unit explore what it means to be someone's friend. Think of experiences you've had with friends to help you answer the following questions about the stories.

1. Why do you think Yvonne agreed to be Nicole's campaign manager in "The Election"?

2. Compare the personalities of Yvonne and Nicole in "The Election."

3. Write three adjectives that describe Olivia in "Whose Band Is It?"

4. Is there a way for the band members in "Whose Band Is It?" to keep their friendship with Olivia and save the band? Explain.

5. Explain why Josephine and Felicia in "The Trouble with Mr. Jones" are such good friends.

6. What do you think Josephine's reaction would have been if she had been treated the way Felicia was by the teacher in "The Trouble with Mr. Jones"?

7. How would you describe Greg and Willie's friendship in "The Accident"?

8. How do you think Willie and Greg could keep their friendship in "The Accident"?

9. How does the diary writer in "Doing Tutor Time" change his attitude toward David during the story?

10. List three possible reasons why Amy came to Lilly with her problem in "A Friend in Need."

11. What do you think would happen to Amy and Lilly's friendship in "A Friend in Need" if Lilly refused to give Amy the money?

12. How are Lucille and Patty alike in "My Turn"? How are they different?

13. How do you think Lucille and Patty's friendship would be affected if Lucille takes Patty's place as the star in "My Turn"?

14. Besides friendship, what does Jimmy have to consider in deciding what to do in "Jimmy's Choice"?

15. How is Jimmy's decision in "Jimmy's Choice" like the tutor's decision in "Doing Tutor Time"?

||||█Thinking About the Ending

All of the main characters in this unit face a conflict with a friend. Think about one of the stories you have read. What do you know about the main character? How does that character feel and act toward his or her friend? What decision must the character make?

Now write an ending to one story in which you show what the character decides to do. Be sure to write what the character says and does, as well as what happens to the friendship as a result of that choice.

A Girl's Best Friend

Erin and Samantha were sitting together in study hall, their heads propped in their hands as they stared at the glorious Jack. Jack smiled. He ran his hand through his thick hair. Erin and Samantha sighed.

"Just to look at him is—" Erin began.

"I know," Samantha said. "I know."

Jack got up, stretched his long legs, and left the room. The girls sighed again.

"At least now I can get some work done," Erin said.

Samantha nodded, then she whispered, "Erin! He's coming back! Wait, he's headed here!"

"*What* is so interesting?" Jack asked, smiling that smile.

"Nothing," said Erin, blushing.

"Nothing," said Samantha. Jack sat down next to them.

"Wait a minute," he said, looking closely at Samantha. "Aren't you in my English class next period?"

"Yes," sighed Samantha, gazing at him. Jack was taken aback for a second. Then he laughed such an infectious laugh that soon Samantha was laughing, too. He walked her to class while Erin trailed behind, delighted for her friend and yet as depressed as she could remember. She was in that English class, too.

Jack walked Samantha to her next class. Then he asked her out. Soon, Erin was listening to daily updates from Samantha about Jack. They'd done this. They were planning that. Erin tried to listen, but she didn't feel much enthusiasm. Not only did she not have Jack, but also she felt like she'd lost her best friend.

"Come on, Erin, it'll be fun. Jack says he has someone he wants you to meet," Samantha was telling Erin.

"I hate being along for the ride," Erin said.

"Listen, Erin, I haven't seen you in days. I miss you. Please? Just for me? I promise you'll have fun."

"All right," Erin said.

They picked her up at 7:00. Erin climbed into the back of the car. By now, she was used to seeing Jack's arm across Samantha's shoulders. "Hey, Erin," he said, turning his head toward her, "my cousin's in town. You'll love him."

Erin smiled politely. When they got to the party, Jack introduced her to his cousin Mason. Like Jack, he was great looking. They talked for a while, and even Erin had to admit that Mason seemed interested.

"Hey, Mason, what did I tell you? Great, huh?" Jack looked at Erin, grinned at his cousin, and walked back to Samantha. The party got louder. Mason and Erin walked outside so they could hear each other talk. He was nice, she had to admit. No Jack, but nice. Jack came out twice to say hi. Then he came out again.

"Hey, Mason, could I borrow Erin for a moment?" Jack asked. He seemed nervous, fidgety.

"Sure," Mason said. "I need to get something to drink anyway."

Jack sat next to Erin on the porch. He didn't say anything for a long time. Then he let out a long sigh.

"Erin, Erin," he said.

What did he want? Was he having trouble with Samantha? It sure didn't look like it to Erin. All Samantha could talk about was how happy she was.

"Erin," Jack said again, "I thought setting you up with Mason would help, but it only made things worse. I'm really attracted to you. I still like Samantha, but I've been thinking about you more and more. I know you're good friends, and this would kill her. I don't know what to do. You tell me. What should I do?"

Erin looked at Jack's troubled face.

"Jack," she began . . .

Daydreamer

"Shalisa, you're incredible," Josh said. "If you hadn't stopped me, I would have stepped right in front of that truck. You saved my life." Josh gazed at her. "I can't believe I never noticed your eyes, or that smile. I—"

"Sha-li-sa!" Josh's handsome face disappeared from her thoughts. Shalisa looked up to see Ms. Gordon glaring at her. "You have got to get out of that world of yours and into this one. I mean now!" Embarrassed, Shalisa gave the teacher a stricken look.

"Ms. Gordon, I—I mean—"

"Shalisa, I can't take this anymore. You have held up this class enough today. Detention. Today. After school."

Shalisa nodded miserably. Everyone was staring at her. She didn't even know what the class had been talking about. Worst of all, Josh was looking at her, too. She wanted to disappear. Shalisa put her head down and pretended to be very busy arranging something on her desk. Maybe she could start really paying attention. Then she would do well in school and win a scholarship to college. Then she'd find out, by accident, that Josh was going to the same college. They'd bump into each other on campus. He'd be surprised. He'd say, "Shalisa, you're here. This is great. I was just thinking about you—" Shalisa shook her head. I can't believe I'm doing this again, and right after I get yelled at, she thought.

"Josh, what's with you today?" Ms. Gordon demanded. "What is with everyone? Josh, you may join Shalisa after school in detention."

Josh was nodding. Shalisa stared at him. He was so nice and so good looking. Shalisa wasn't sure, but she thought he was interested in Mandy. She'd seen them together. After class, Shalisa put her head down and headed out. She didn't want to talk to anybody.

Shalisa walked into detention after school and took one of the two seats left. The whole school must have been in trouble, she thought, as she looked at the nearly full detention room. Then Josh came in and took the last seat, next to her. Shalisa's heart began to pound. She looked down. She didn't know what she could possibly say to him.

He didn't say anything to her, either. He got out his algebra book and began to read. Shalisa got out hers, too. They were in the same class, but she didn't think Josh even knew that.

Time went quickly. Here, Shalisa could daydream all she wanted. "Just give me a hug," Josh was saying in her daydream. "Where shall we go Saturday night?" Shalisa sighed, brushed Josh's shoulder accidentally and was so flustered that she dropped her pencil. They both stooped down to pick it up and bumped heads. Then their eyes met. The next thing Shalisa knew . . .

*S*urprise Attack

Dear Diary,

I haven't written in a diary for years, but I need someone to talk to, and I'm not ready to talk to a real person. I guess I'm afraid I'll be told to do something that I don't want to do yet.

William was late again tonight. He was supposed to come by at 8:00, but he didn't show up till 10:00 and it was too late to go out, so we just went for a walk.

I was so mad at him that I couldn't speak for a long time. This is the third time this week that he's been late. He said he was just hanging out with his friends and didn't know the time, but he always says that. He said he was really sorry, but it didn't matter to me.

I yelled at him for a long time. I couldn't stop shouting, and I just stood there on the sidewalk and yelled and yelled until he told me to be quiet. He begged me, but I couldn't stop yelling. I saw him talking to his old girlfriend in school last week, and ever since then I've been worried he's been seeing her. I guess I was really jealous.

Finally, William hit me. He just hauled off and punched me right in the face, and I couldn't believe it. It shut me up, all right, but not for long. I stopped yelling and started to cry. I could tell that William was surprised that he had hit me. He kept saying, "I'm sorry, I'm sorry." I could tell he meant it, but I didn't care.

I just wanted to run away, so that's what I did. I raced down the street, got home, and ran straight to my room. I looked in the mirror. My face was already starting to swell up, and I could tell my eye was going to be black.

What am I going to tell people, and what will my

parents think? What are the kids at school going to say?

I wonder if it was all my fault. I wonder if he would have hit me if I hadn't yelled so much. But I had a right to yell if he was with his old girlfriend. I'm so confused.

I know that my parents will make me break up with William if I tell them. They will say that nobody should hit another person, and they won't care why it happened.

"If someone hits you once, he'll hit you again," they will tell me. But I wonder if that's true. I wonder if William will hit me again if I don't break up with him.

My face is swelling up, and I'll have to say something to my parents. I guess I'll tell them that . . .

he Photo

Dear Diary,

I'm writing to you because I desperately need to sort something out. I have a new boyfriend—he's wonderful, his name is James, and I like him better than any boyfriend I've ever had. But I have a serious problem.

Dorrie came to visit last month. My parents had never met her before, but I told them a lot about her before she came. I mentioned that she was my best friend at camp, and I told them about all the things we did together and how much fun we had. But I didn't tell them that she is black because my parents are very prejudiced. They won't admit it, but they are, and I was afraid that they wouldn't let her visit us if they knew. I knew they would have to be nice to her if she was our guest, but after she left, my mother said, "Don't ever do that to us again!"

"Do what?" I muttered angrily because I understood

what she was referring to.

"You know what," she answered, and then she turned and walked away.

While Dorrie was visiting, we took pictures. I took some pictures of Dorrie, and Dorrie took some of me. Then my mom took a few of the two of us together.

James and I started going out the day after Dorrie left. I was so happy to be with him that I forgot all about the roll of film. Then one day last week, I found the roll. It had one picture left on it, so I took a picture of James.

Then I took the roll to the film store.

Now, Diary, here is the problem. My mother found the receipt for the pictures. She picked them up and studied them carefully. She asked me who the boy in the picture was. I realized that she was referring to James. I also realized that she would never let me go out with him if I told her the truth. But I hate lying. I hated lying about Dorrie before she came.

I know it is my mom's fault for being prejudiced, but

it is also my fault for being such a coward.

I want to tell her the truth, no matter what she says, but what if it means I never get to see James again?

I don't know what to do. Wait! Maybe I do know now. I think I will . . .

Letter Across Time

Samantha's parents had bought the desk for her at a garage sale. The woman who had the sale was moving into an apartment. She was selling most of her furniture.

The desk was beautiful. The wood was old and well cared for. Samantha pulled down the rolled front of the desk. Inside were tiny drawers. She put her hand into each one to see if there was anything there. She found a pencil stub in the first drawer. Then she put her hand into another drawer. Nothing there. In the third drawer, her fingers felt the edge of a piece of paper. She pulled it out. It was an old letter, unopened and postmarked 1941. It was addressed to the woman who had owned the desk.

On an impulse, Samantha put on her coat and went back to the woman's house. The sale was still in progress. The woman was sitting in a chair on the front lawn, surrounded by furniture. Her white hair was in a perfect knot. She was dressed simply. Hesitantly, Samantha approached her.

"Um, ma'am?" she said.

The woman looked up. "Yes?" she responded.

In a rush, Samantha said, "Um, we bought—I mean,

my folks bought—your desk. I was looking at it, and I found this." She held out the letter.

The woman, who had looked amused at Samantha's rush of words, took the envelope and examined it. Suddenly, her face softened. "Jeremy," she murmured.

Samantha was dying to know who Jeremy was. She waited for a minute while the woman stared at the envelope. She seemed almost afraid to open it.

"I hate to be nosy," Samantha said at last, "but who's Jeremy?"

The woman laughed. "An old friend. An old, old, friend." Samantha looked at her expectantly. "Well, actually, there is a story to this letter," she continued. "Jeremy was my first love. Then I fell in love with another boy who was going off to World War II. We married, and he died in the war. I never remarried. I was too ashamed of the way I'd treated Jeremy to try to find him." She smoothed the letter. "He gave me this letter before I was married. I never read it. I couldn't bear to, so I put it away. I had forgotten all about it."

Slowly, she opened the letter and read it while Samantha watched. When she finished, the woman bowed her head. Then Samantha realized she was crying.

The woman looked up at her. "He wrote, 'Remember: I will always love you,'" she said sadly.

Samantha looked at the woman's tear-streaked face. "We can find him! I know we can!" she cried.

The woman shook her head. "It's too late. Look at me. I'm old. I would rather have my memories than be disappointed. He's probably married. I've changed. No," she said, shaking her head, "it would never work."

"Oh, don't say that!" Samantha said. "We'll find him!"

"No, I couldn't," the woman said.

"You must!" Samantha said. "You may be missing the chance of your life!" The woman looked at her for a long moment and then said . . .

Longing, excitement, doubt—they're all part of being in love. When you're in love, you often don't know exactly what to say or what to do. Suddenly, you're dealing with feelings and emotions you've never had before. There is also that soaring sense that someone really likes you, that someone would rather be with you than with anyone else.

Along with feelings of happiness can come feelings of doubt, though. Does the other person really like me? How should I act? What does it mean when he walks away like that? What does it mean when she says that she wants time alone? Everyone has faced these uncertainties.

The stories in this unit deal with romance. Even if you've never had that experience, you know what it's like to feel unsure of yourself. You probably also know what it's like to really like someone and to hope he or she feels the same way. Use your own experiences and those of your friends to help you answer these questions about the stories in this unit.

1. In "A Girl's Best Friend," Samantha and Erin consider themselves to be best friends. What happens to threaten their friendship?

2. Do you think Erin is a good friend? Find an example in "A Girl's Best Friend" to support your answer.

3. Based on what you know about Shalisa in "Daydreamer," do you think that she and Josh could have a good relationship? Explain.

4. What do you think Josh's opinion is of Shalisa in "Daydreamer"? Explain.

5. Do you think William in "Surprise Attack" is likely to hit the writer again? Explain your answer.

6. How are the situations different for the writers in "Surprise Attack" and "The Photo"? How are they similar?

7. Describe the writer in "The Photo."

8. If the writer in "The Photo" tells her mother the truth, she will also have to explain her mother's attitude to James. Write how you think the diary writer should explain her situation to him.

9. How do you think the older woman in "Letter Across Time" feels about Jeremy? How can you tell?

10. Imagine that the older woman in "Letter Across Time" is on her way to see Jeremy. What do you think she is feeling?

IIIII THINKING ABOUT THE ENDING

The characters in these stories face problems in love ranging from a parent's bigotry to caring for the same person. As you think about writing an ending for one of these stories, think about what you know about the main character. How would this person resolve his or her problem? What would this person consider before making a decision?

Now write an ending to the story. Show both the decision the character makes and how he or she makes it. Also show what happens to the relationship between the characters as a result of the decision.

Almost Perfect

"So you have a class with him, right?" Brenda asked Magda.

"Uh-huh. He's in my theater class." Magda was concentrating more on her lunch than on the conversation.

"Well?" Brenda looked at her.

"Well what?"

"Is he smart?" Brenda practically yelled.

"Of course he's smart. The guy is almost perfect."

Magda was trying not to sound as impressed as she was, but it was hard. Christopher Ferguson was only a freshman at Denbigh High School, but almost everyone knew who he was.

Brenda stared off into space. "A great basketball player, smart, and incredibly good looking. He really is perfect—well, almost perfect. I mean he is still a freshman."

"So what?" Magda asked, eating her sandwich.

Brenda looked stunned. "So what? The guy is a freshman. That means he is a social nothing. Magda, we're seniors. Freshmen do not count."

"Relax, OK?" Magda replied. "You make it sound like I'll drop dead if I say the guy's name out loud."

All I ever hear is how great Christopher Ferguson would be if he weren't a freshman, Magda thought. She didn't understand what the big deal about freshmen was.

"You don't have to worry. I won't embarrass you," Magda said. "Christopher Ferguson doesn't even exist as far as I'm concerned, OK?"

Brenda looked relieved. "OK. See you after school." Smiling, she grabbed her books and left.

Magda took her time gathering up her things. I don't get it, she thought. He seems like such a nice guy. No one even wants to date any of the senior guys because all they care about is whether everyone thinks they're cool. Everyone knows Chris, and he still acts like a human being.

Magda sighed and walked into theater class.

"Today, you'll be discussing the final project," Mr. Hockman said. "I've assigned groups of two who will be performing a scene from the play of their choice." Great, Magda thought. I'll probably end up with some geeky guy. She turned her attention to Mr. Hockman.

". . . third group, Anna and Joe," Mr. Hockman droned on. "Fourth group, Magda and Christopher. Fifth group . . ." Magda stopped listening. Had she heard him correctly? Yes, Christopher was smiling and walking toward her desk.

"Hey, I'm glad we're partners," he said.

"Yeah," Magda replied with a smile.

"I have to leave early today for a basketball game. Can I call you tonight to talk about this?" Christopher asked.

"Sure," she answered. "Good luck."

Later that evening, the phone rang and a polite voice on the other end said, "Magda? This is Christopher."

"Oh, hi," Magda said, trying to sound casual. "So, uh, what play do you think we should work on?"

For a moment, there was silence. Suddenly, Chris blurted out, "Magda, I'm really glad you're my partner because there's something I wanted to talk to you about. There's a dance on Friday. Will you go with me?"

Magda was shocked. Christopher Ferguson is actually asking me out on a date! she thought excitedly. I can't wait to tell Brenda! But then Magda remembered Brenda's words at lunch.

Brenda was right—all of Magda's friends would make fun of her for going out with a freshman. But how could she turn down a date with a guy she really liked?

"Magda? Are you still there?" Christopher asked nervously.

"Yeah, I'm here. About Friday night . . .

Losing It All

June 1

Dear Diary,

You'll never guess what happened to me today. I went into the stationery store to get Mom a birthday card, and I found this amazing book about diets that guarantees a loss of at least 10 pounds a week! I've decided it's time for me to shed all this fat and become beautiful.

According to the charts, I'm 42 pounds overweight. I don't know how I let myself get like this. I guess I just became really depressed when we moved last year. It was so hard leaving my friends. I sure hope this diet works.

June 8

Dear Diary,

It really works! I can't believe it! I lost 10 pounds in one week! At this rate, I'll be a new person by September. Starting tomorrow, I'm trying another diet in the book. It says that I'll lose pounds and inches. I can't wait to see the results.

Dear Diary,

Hooray! Five more pounds off! It would have been more, but I snacked a little. Anyway, I devised a surefire way to keep from cheating. I'm going shopping for all new clothes, size eight. That way I won't have any choice but to stay on this diet.

Dear Diary,

I feel awful. I cheated like crazy yesterday. I guess it was because one of my friends from my old school called. She said she wasn't going to be able to make it down for the 4th of July weekend. I just got the feeling she really didn't want to take time out to visit me. Anyway, once I started, I just couldn't stop eating. I gained 4 pounds!

Dear Diary,

Today, I heard some girls talking about a way to pig out and still stay skinny. All you have to do is stick your finger down your throat. The food will come back up. It's gross, but nothing could be worse than gaining weight.

Dear Diary,

Twenty-four pounds off in one month! Not bad, huh? I'm halfway there. It's getting harder, though. Every time I pass an ice cream shop, my mouth waters. At night, sometimes I cry. But at least I'm doing something about it. Now if I cheat, I just stick my fingers down my throat. It works like a charm.

Dear Diary,

I can't believe how much I pigged out at the family barbecue. I ate EVERYTHING. Of course, I threw it all up. But there was so much food left, I ended up eating all over again. After I threw up the second time, my stomach burned. I've got to be good for the rest of the week.

Dear Diary,

Mom caught me in the bathroom throwing up! We were all at my aunt's house for a family dinner. I stuffed myself; then I sneaked into the bathroom and started to throw up. When I was almost finished, Mom walked in and caught me. I was so embarrassed. I told her . . .

Hold-up

Cobra opened his eyes slowly and squinted. The morning sun was blinding him, so he pulled the covers over his head and tried to go back to sleep. But it was no use. Somebody was in the living room, hollering loudly.

"There has to be a way to stop it!" the voice shouted. "Shhh, Benjamin," Cobra heard his mother say. "You'll wake up everybody."

Mr. Jefferson lowered his voice, but Cobra could still hear him shouting. "Somebody broke the side window of my store last night. Every day, it's something different, but it's always those gangs. This neighborhood is being destroyed by those lunatic gangs."

Cobra threw off the covers and sat up because Mr. Jefferson's words reminded him of something. Today was his first day as a member of the Ravens, and he was supposed to meet them in 15 minutes. He hoped that the Ravens hadn't smashed Benjamin Jefferson's window because he liked Mr. Jefferson. He'd known the man ever since he was 10 years old, and Benjamin had always been good to him. Sometimes, Cobra even helped him out in his grocery store.

Cobra dressed quickly and raced through the living room.

"Whoa, David!" Mr. Jefferson laughed. "What's the hurry?"

But Cobra didn't stop. Cobra was his new name. He had chosen it the night before, and from now on he would not answer to anything but Cobra.

Fifteen minutes later, he was in the schoolyard surrounded by the other Ravens.

"Are you ready?" the leader asked Cobra.

Cobra was ready, but he didn't know what he was supposed to be ready for.

"It's initiation day," one of the other Ravens said. "It's the day you get to show what's inside you."

Cobra narrowed his eyes and shoved his hands into his pockets. He was scared, and the only thing that was inside him was terror. He was completely in it now, and there was no way out. He had to do whatever they said.

For a moment, he wondered how he had gotten into this. He had just been hanging out, and they wouldn't take no for an answer. Join the Ravens, they had insisted, and in the end he didn't have a choice.

He glanced at his feet and waited for them to tell him what he was supposed to do for his initiation. He hoped it wouldn't be too bad.

"There are no alarms in the place," the leader was saying. "We found that out last night when we threw a rock through a window."

Cobra's eyes widened for a second and then narrowed again. So they had tossed that rock through Mr. Jefferson's window. Now Cobra was really scared.

The leader moved closer to him and muttered, "So all you have to do is rob this grocery store."

"Whose?" Cobra whispered, but he knew which store they meant.

"Jefferson's," the leader told him. There's no alarm, and he's not there after 6:00. Just open the window and take the money."

Cobra felt sick as he remembered all the candy Mr. Jefferson had given him and the time that Mr. Jefferson had hidden him when some boys were after him.

The Ravens were watching him carefully. He knew what they did to gang members who didn't go along. They broke their fingers, and sometimes they broke their arms.

Cobra made his face appear blank, nodded, and said, "I'll do whatever you say." He thought long and hard and he knew what he had to do. Cobra decided to . . .

New Shoes

"Mom, I know they're expensive," Jimmy said. "But I really, really want them. I could play such great basketball if I had them." Jimmy did an imaginary dribble, spun, tossed the imaginary ball, and felt it slide cleanly through the hoop.

His mother was looking at him with a mixture of exasperation and sadness.

"Look, Jimmy, I don't know where those friends of yours get the money for those expensive shoes, but we can't afford them. One pair of those shoes would feed us for three weeks. Three weeks! I don't know how you can even suggest it. You know the money situation."

Jimmy sat down and crossed his arms, kicking at the bottom of the table leg. It was always the same. A constant drumbeat. Not enough money. Not enough money. Just once he'd like to hear his mother say, "Oh, honey, you want a new pair of shoes? Of course. Here's a hundred dollars. You just go right out and get them."

He couldn't even get a job. There weren't any. If he only had the money. He could see himself walking down the halls at school, wearing a pair of those high-topped HighLanders. The guys who had them said they were unreal. They said those shoes helped them jump higher than ever before.

Even though he knew the answer wouldn't change, Jimmy asked his mother again the next week. "Couldn't I just eat less for a while?" he pleaded. "We could save the money that way."

His mother bit her lip and looked at him. He could tell she was upset. He could see the pain in her eyes. "Honey," she said softly, "please don't do this to me. You know we don't have the money. Please don't ask again."

Jimmy didn't ask again. In a few weeks, the guys talked less about the shoes. In a couple of months, they were talking about a new kind of shoe designed in a completely new way. They were unbelievable, kids said. Hardly anyone was wearing HighLanders anymore. The kids who did got teased, as if they wore those stupid shoes because they didn't know what was going on. It was better to wear regular sneakers, in a way. That way, you could just pretend to be beyond all the hype.

Then it was October—Jimmy's birthday. He was having some of the guys over for cake before they all went to the movies. He got some great stuff—CDs and clothes—from his friends. Then his mom gave him a present, her eyes sparkling.

"Come on, Jimmy, open it," she said eagerly.

He did. Inside was a pair of HighLanders. Jimmy stared at them. His friends were quiet. His mom looked at him happily, unaware of the small smiles his friends were giving one another.

"Put them on, Jimmy, put them on," she said eagerly.

He couldn't wear these shoes. Nobody was wearing them. Everyone would laugh at him. Maybe he could pretend they didn't fit. Then he became a little angry at his mom. Didn't she know anything? He looked at her, all smiling and proud of herself, and he was sad because she'd saved up to buy these stupid shoes. Maybe he could just return them and get some great shoes.

"Can you believe it? I found them on sale," she said to him, all smiles. He smiled weakly back. So he probably couldn't take them back. Jimmy looked at his friends. Then he looked at his mother and said . . .

The Ride

Little James leaned against the wall and slid his hands into his pockets. He was late, but he didn't want to leave. It was fun hanging out on the corner with his buddies. Sophie was going to be mad, though.

So let her be mad, Little James thought. She's been mad before, and she's always gotten over it.

"Want to shoot some pool, James?" his friend Ork asked.

Little James shook his head. "I promised Sophie I'd be at her place by 9:00, and I'm already late. I guess I should head out."

But he didn't move. It was too nice there with all his friends. His friend Frank opened another beer and tried to pass it to James, but James wasn't interested. Sophie wouldn't like it if he'd been drinking when he arrived, and Little James wasn't ready to give up on Sophie. He knew she was good for him. Sophie kept him out of trouble, most of the time.

Frank downed the beer and opened another one. This was his fifth beer tonight, and he was showing it. Little James said goodbye to Ork and started to walk away.

"Where're you going?" Frank slurred.

"Sophie's waiting," Little James explained.

Frank's head fell back against the wall, and his eyes slid closed. He eventually opened them again and tried to focus on James.

"Sophie, Sophie, Sophie," Frank groaned. "That's all you ever talk about."

He passed the beer to Ork and watched as Ork took a sip and tried to pass it to James.

"Come on, Little Man," Ork said. "Join us."

They were all watching James, so he took one quick sip and passed it back. Then he turned and started to walk away. He could hear them chuckling behind his back.

"Hey, James!" Frank hollered suddenly.

James stopped and turned.

"How about a ride?" Frank asked as he staggered toward him.

Frank stumbled drunkenly past him and climbed onto his motorcycle. Then he patted the seat behind him gently and grinned. "Hop on," he mumbled. "I'm going your way." James studied Frank's sleepy eyes. There was no way that he was getting on that bike, but how was he going to refuse?

He turned and looked at his friends. They were watching him carefully.

"Don't worry," Ork said, laughing. "We won't tell Sophie."

"What does Sophie have to do with this?" James asked.

"Get on," Frank said. "I shall deliver you to Sophie's doorstep personally, in the nick of time."

Frank slammed the pedal and gave it some gas. Then he grinned stupidly at James and patted the seat again.

James shuffled his feet. He didn't know what to do. Sophie would definitely be mad that he was late, but he wondered how she would feel if he died getting there.

He didn't want to be dead, but he didn't want to be laughed at either. It was very confusing.

"Let's go, James," Frank repeated impatiently. James looked at the motorcycle and made up his mind. He . . .

The Book

Big Red stomped on the gas pedal and gave his motorcycle some gas. Only five more miles to the library. It was a long way to go for a book, but he had to do it. Big Red really wanted to find out more about dolphins. They were as intelligent as people, but they were different, too.

Big Red hid the book under his pillow. He didn't want anyone in the gang to know about the book because if they knew, they'd tease him. They might even beat him up.

He met the gang at noon the next day, and one of them asked, "Where were you yesterday? "

"Sick," Big Red said. He wished that he could tell them that he'd really been at the library. He wished that he could get out of this gang, but these guys were like family.

"Well, we're in serious trouble," the leader explained. "There was a fight yesterday, and somebody was hurt. The cops are on their way right now."

"I was at the library and I can prove it," Big Red wanted to say. But he didn't say it because he remembered the gang's motto: A gang sticks together, no matter what.

Big Red knew he could tell the police about the library, and he could show them the book. He could prove that he had been out of town. But would his buddies throw him out of the gang if he told them? Maybe the cops would let them all off, but that was doubtful. Someone had been hurt, and they needed to make arrests.

Big Red straddled his bike and closed his eyes. He hadn't done anything, and he didn't want to go to jail, but what could he do? There's only one thing to do, he finally decided . . .

IIIII Thinking About the Stories

Everyone has to deal with peer pressure. The pressure may be as simple as not wearing a piece of clothing because you're afraid your friends will laugh, or it may be as serious as being dared to do something you know is dangerous. How far someone will go to please friends and how far someone else will go to be accepted are decisions every person has to make at some point. How do people decide how much to let their friends influence them?

In this unit, characters have to choose between doing things they think are wrong or dangerous and defying their friends. You have probably had to make choices like these and have watched your friends make similar choices. Use your experience and your understanding of the characters in the stories to answer these questions.

1. What do you think Brenda's reaction would be if Magda decided to date Chris in "Almost Perfect"?

2. Imagine you are Magda in "Almost Perfect." Make a list of reasons to date and not date Chris.

3. Describe the writer in "Losing It All."

4. Explain why you think the writer in "Losing It All" chose to try to control her weight in this way.

5. Explain the relationship between Benjamin Jefferson and Cobra in "Hold Up."

6. Why do you think Cobra became friends with the Ravens in "Hold Up"?

7. What do you think is more important to Jimmy in "New Shoes," his relationship with his mother or his relationship with his friends? Explain.

8. In the story "New Shoes," can you think of a way for Jimmy to make his mother happy without embarrassing himself in front of his friends? Explain.

9. What are the differences and similarities in the situations the main characters face in "New Shoes" and "The Ride"?

10. What influence do you think Sophie has had on Little James's behavior in "The Ride"?

11. Why does Big Red think the gang members in "The Book" would give him a hard time if they knew he had been at the library?

12. What do you think would happen to Big Red in "The Book" if he told the truth? What do you think would happen to him if he lied?

From being rejected to possibly being hurt, the main characters in these stories face consequences for sticking with their friends. In some cases, the characters know their friends are wrong. In other stories, it's a choice of being laughed at for making an unpopular choice. Think about the choices a character has to make in one of these stories. What might cause the character to take one course of action?

Write an ending for one of these stories. Make sure to include the reaction the character's friends have to his or her decision and how the decision may affect their friendship.

*L*oyalties

Tracey's first thought when she woke up Saturday morning was, "Tomorrow, Su will be gone." Saturday meant no school, but Tracey had been dreading this particular Saturday for the last month. Tomorrow morning, her best friend Su would get on a plane to France and begin a new life. Most of Su's family was in Europe, and her parents had scraped together the last of their savings so that she could join them.

"Tracey, are you awake?" her mother yelled.

"Yeah, I'm up," Tracey replied, under the covers.

"If you want to spend the day with Su, you'd better get up and finish that paper."

Reluctantly, Tracey rolled out of bed. She grabbed her notebook and settled into her desk chair. Su's last day, and here I am finishing up my English midterm, she mumbled to herself. The group project was due the next day, and Tracey was eager to finish her part and deliver it to Rebecca, the group chairperson.

Two hours later, Tracey got off the bus at the stop in front of Rebecca's apartment. When no one answered her knocks at the door, she left her work in the mailbox.

Done, finally! Now I have the rest of the day to hang out with Su, she said to herself as the bus pulled up to the curb. By 11:15, she was sitting in Su's bedroom, watching her pile clothes into a suitcase.

"My parents want you to go out to dinner with us as a kind of special farewell," Su said sadly.

"Of course I'll come to dinner," Tracey replied.

Su smiled. "So are you glad that project's done?"

"Well, my part's finished, anyway," Tracey replied. "I hope Rebecca found it in the mailbox."

"Doesn't your answering machine have one of those remote things that lets you check your messages from somewhere else?" Su asked. Tracey nodded. "If Rebecca didn't find it, she'd leave a message on your machine, right?"

"I think I'll check," said Tracey. She dialed her number and punched the buttons to access her messages.

"Tracey, it's Rebecca. We've got some major problems with the project. Plan to have dinner over here tonight because it's going to take at least that long to fix this thing. Call me back as soon as you can."

Returning to the room, Su announced, "Mom says we're going to that Mexican place near the mall for dinner."

Dinner with Su! In her concern over the project, Tracey had almost forgotten about it. If I go to Rebecca's, we'll have to say goodbye now because Su will be busy for the rest of the night, she thought. I can just tell Rebecca that I didn't get the message till I got home, and then it was too late. But Tracey felt guilty thinking about that. That's pretty unfair, she thought. Besides, I need a decent grade on the project. She started to bite her nails.

"Tracey, what's wrong?" Su asked.

Tracey answered . . .

*T*he Choice

Lewis was sweeping the floor in the principal's office when the school secretary, Kelly, poked her head in.

"There are two burnt-out lights in Mr. Gann's room," she said. "Could you take care of that tonight?"

"Sure," said Lewis. "Where's Mr. Gann?"

"Room 4," Kelly answered. "I don't think you have the key to that room yet, but I doubt that you'll need it. Mr. Gann is probably still here."

"Late worker, huh?" Lewis asked.

"Oh, Mr. Gann is our star teacher," Kelly explained with a smile. "We give him all our tough kids, and he does wonders with them."

"That's great," Lewis said. He put away the broom and started for the door. "I'll take care of those lights now," he said. I can vacuum the gym tonight."

"Thank you, Lewis," Kelly said. "That would be terrific. . . . By the way, Mrs. Manske said you've been doing a great job."

Lewis grinned. It never hurt to have the principal like your work. Lewis liked Everett High. So far, this new job was going well.

Lewis got a couple of long fluorescent bulbs from the storeroom and carried them to Room 4. Inside the classroom, the teacher was working at his desk.

Lewis opened the door. The teacher looked up.

"Hi," Lewis said. "I'm the new janitor. I—" He stopped and stared at the man behind the desk.

Lewis flashed back to a hot night in June seven years earlier. He was working as a cashier at Minute Mart. It was almost 1 A.M., and he was just about to put the closed sign on the door.

A guy had come in, wearing a red T-shirt. He was about Lewis's age. He'd picked out a few things; then he'd walked up to the counter and paid. Lewis had opened the register to give him his change. Then when he'd looked up, the guy'd had a gun in his hand.

The guy stared at him coldly. Lewis had felt a frozen spot in his chest, as if he could already feel the bullet.

"Don't close the register," the man had demanded. "Put it all in here." He'd pushed a bag across the counter.

Lewis didn't remember how he got all the money into the bag. He didn't remember much else that happened after that. But he knew he'd remember that face behind the gun forever. It was a thin face, with one eye looking straight ahead and the other eye looking in a slightly different direction.

"They never found out who did it," Lewis said to the teacher sitting before him.

"Excuse me?" the teacher asked.

"Minute Mart. Seven years ago," Lewis said. "You robbed the place. You pulled a gun on me!"

The teacher's mouth moved, but no words came out. He was the one, all right. Lewis could see the guilt in his face.

"They never found out who did it," Lewis continued. "But they're going to now!" He would call the police, and this guy would finally end up behind bars—where he belonged!

"Wait!" the teacher exclaimed. "That night I got away, but I had this feeling—a strong feeling—that next time my luck would run out. I was sick of my life. After that night, I changed. I turned things around."

Lewis shook his head. "You've got dues to pay."

The teacher said, "I've paid them! I mean, I'm doing a lot of good here. The kids work hard in my class. When I tell them they have to stay in school, they believe me. Maybe because they know it got me off the street. Because of me, they know they can do it, too."

Lewis thought back to that night seven years ago. The day after the holdup, he quit. Once, he had dreamed of having his own store. The dream had ended that night.

The teacher continued, "If you turn me in, a lot of these kids will get into gangs and drugs. I can promise you that."

Lewis looked at the light bulbs on the table where he'd set them down. He could change the light bulbs and leave, or he could make that phone call.

The teacher's voice was almost a whisper. "What are you going to do?" he asked.

Lewis thought hard for a minute and then he . . .

Rush Hour

Kyle looked down at his watch and then up at the line in front of him. He was much closer to the token booth than he had been five minutes ago, but there were still ten people ahead of him.

It was rush hour, and the subway was filled with people anxious to get to work or school on time. Kyle was no exception. He could hear the warning Mr. Allen had given him after class the day before: "If you're late just one more time, Kyle, you're suspended from the football team for two weeks."

Kyle knew Mr. Allen wasn't kidding. He looked impatiently toward the front of the line.

The subway was full of noises—radios set at high volume, babies crying, people shouting. In the middle of all the commotion, Kyle could suddenly hear one sound very clearly. Tap tap tap. . . . The sound echoed off the floor. Tap tap tap. . . . Kyle could hear it coming closer. It was almost right behind him now.

When he turned around he saw a pair of large, mirrored sunglasses. They were sitting on the nose of a very tall man with slicked-back hair. Kyle's eyes moved downward to the long, thin cane in the man's hand. The man moved the cane in front of himself in a wide circle as he walked forward.

He realized the man was searching for the token line. He won't be able to find it with all these people around, Kyle thought. For a moment, he watched the man move slowly forward. Most people moved out of his way as they rushed past, but some pushed against him in their hurry, moving him farther away from the line.

Kyle started to reach out for the man's suit jacket. I'll just tell him to head a little to his right, he thought.

Just as Kyle began to stretch out his arm, the man's cane touched the edge of the token booth along which the line had formed. Satisfied that the man had found his way, Kyle turned back to the line. He checked his watch again—7:32. I can catch the 7:40. I'll make it to class with two minutes to spare, he said to himself.

Suddenly, Kyle yelped, and looked down to find a white stick poking his big toe.

"Sorry if I scared you," the man said. "I'm just glad I finally found the line. Do you know where I catch the 7:38 train to 18th Street and 6th Avenue?"

"Sure," Kyle replied. "You have to go down to the third platform. Be careful not to get on the express. It doesn't stop until 12th Street."

The man smiled sheepishly. "Are you going near that platform?" he asked. "I haven't lived here for too long, and people are usually in too much of a rush to help me."

Kyle looked at his watch. He had four minutes to catch the train, or he would definitely be late for class. If he stayed to show the man the right train, he'd never make the 7:40 to school. But how could he just leave this man alone in the subway station? Then he thought about Mr. Allen's warning again.

Kyle looked at his watch and then at the cane in the man's hand. He turned and . . .

The Invitation

Lee leaned back against the wall, watching the party and thinking that it was about time to go. His best friend, Brad, would be finishing his shift at the gas station at 10, and Lee had said he'd give him a ride home.

Across the room was Brad's girlfriend, Nikki. She had come with a bunch of kids from school. They stood in a tight circle, half talking, half dancing. She was cute, kind of skinny, but with a lot of energy. A couple of times Lee had gone to the movies with Nikki and Brad, but she'd never paid him much attention. He figured he was too quiet for her, too boring.

One of the boys was telling a joke, but Nikki wasn't listening. She was looking across the room—at him.

Lee turned away quickly and started to talk to the guy next to him. A minute later, Nikki was standing right next to him, her bright mouth smiling wide.

"Hi, Lee," she said.

"Hi," Lee replied. He glanced over at the guy he'd been talking to, but he'd disappeared.

Nikki asked, "Who did you come with tonight?"

"Nobody," Lee answered. "I just came by myself." She was even cuter close up, he thought. He imagined walking down the halls at school with Nikki at his side. Stop it, he told himself. She's Brad's girlfriend.

Nikki laughed softly. "No, no, no. You must have come with somebody." She twirled a piece of her hair, her eyes dancing.

Lee felt almost dizzy, as if he'd stepped off a fast elevator.

She continued, "You have a girlfriend, right?"

Lee laughed. "Wrong," he said.

"Are you sure?" Nikki asked.

"Sure," Lee responded. Why couldn't he think of anything interesting to say?

A space cleared in the crowd, and several couples started to dance.

"Do you want to dance?" she asked. She sounded almost shy now.

He glanced at his watch. "I'd better go," he said. "I'm supposed to be somewhere at 10:00."

Her face fell. She looked as if she'd lost something. Lee hated to have her look that way. He wanted to see her laugh. He imagined dancing with her, holding her close. Then he imagined Brad seeing the two of them together and the hurt, angry look on his best friend's face. He should leave right now.

Nikki saw him hesitate. "You're not going to leave the party now, are you?" she asked.

It was time to decide. Lee could go get his jacket, or he could stay with Nikki. He made his decision and . . .

*O*ne Day Long Ago

"We're seriously broke, Z!" Frazier sighed loudly. "We have no money. We can't even afford dinner."

Underground Z glanced at his drummer and shrugged. He knew the band didn't have any money because his manager, Jake, had been telling him that for weeks.

"So how's the new song?" Frazier asked.

"It's fine," Underground Z said. "No, it's more than fine. It's the best song I've ever written."

"Good, because we need an enormous hit," Frazier replied. "If we don't have a hit soon, there won't be enough money to go on the road."

The song was finally finished, and it was better than fine. Z called it "One Day Long Ago," and it was magnificent. As soon as Jake arrived, Z planned to sing it to the band. "You ready?" Z asked, when Jake arrived.

"I'm ready," Jake answered. "This song better be as brilliant as you said." Z grabbed the mike and started to sing. He sang the words clearly and slowly. He had worked so hard on the lyrics that he wanted everyone to understand them perfectly.

He sang about the mouse in the garbage, the cop on the corner, and the ten-dollar bill on the sidewalk. But when he got to the part about his father leaving, he slowed down and closed his eyes. It had been so hard to write about the day his father walked out forever, but it was even harder to sing about it.

When he was finished, he opened his eyes and looked at his band. They were smiling and nodding, and he could tell that they liked the song. Jake didn't say anything for a long time. He was frowning.

"It's nice, Z," he said at last. "I liked the mouse. But it needs a punch."

"A punch?" Z repeated. "What does that mean?"

"It means that you just have to punch it up and give it a beat. We want people to dance to this," Jake explained.

"You want a hit," Z groaned.

"That's right. I want a hit, and I don't like the sad part. I want a happy song. The hit's there, if you cut the sad part and jazz it up."

When Jake was gone, Z sat down and stared at his hands. He felt terrible. He didn't want to change the song. He had worked on it for months, and it was perfect.

"Maybe he's right, Z," Frazier said. "It could be our hit single if you cut the part about the guy leaving. You could just make it a song that would make people happy."

"But it's not that kind of song," Z whispered sadly.

"We need the money," Frazier whispered back. "If we don't get the money soon, we'll have to sell the equipment, and then we won't have a band."

Z knew that Frazier was right, but this song meant everything to him. What could he do? He thought about the song all night, and the next morning he called the band members together.

"Here's what I've decided," he told them . . .

*T*he Secret

Dear Diary,

You are the only one that I can tell my secret to. The nice thing is that I finally have a job! I take tickets for the octopus ride at the amusement park, and it's really easy. All I have to do is hold out my hand and collect the tickets. The amusement park is so much fun. My friends come by and see me all the time. Best of all is the money. My family really needs it. Mom lost her job last month, and Dad doesn't make enough to support all of us. So the whole family is happy that I have this wonderful new job.

But there is one problem, and it's a big one. The problem is the people who work on the ride. I watched them put the ride together, and they were laughing and joking the whole time. They weren't paying attention to what they were doing. They forgot to screw in one of the bolts, and then, when they realized what they had done, they just laughed about it. But they didn't fix it, so I'm really scared. The owner is nice, but all he cares about is money. When I told him about the loose screw, he just laughed. He said to mind my own business. But what if something happens to one of the cars, and someone is hurt? If that happened and I didn't try to do something, then it would be my fault too, wouldn't it?

I have to do something, but I have no idea what to do. I really need the money from this job. I guess I will . . .

The Third Street Beggar

On the way to school, Daniel passed a beggar. The man sat against the stop sign at Third Street. As Daniel stood at the corner, waiting for the light to change, the man grabbed his shirt.

"Hey," the beggar said, "you got a quarter?"

Daniel couldn't believe the man had touched him. He slapped the beggar's hand away. Daniel couldn't stand those people who hung out on the streets doing nothing, asking people for money. Why didn't they clean themselves up and get jobs? Anybody could work at a fast-food restaurant and make a few dollars. Nobody had to live on the street, begging from people who work for their money. There was no excuse for that man.

To avoid the beggar, Daniel walked a different way to school the next day, but it was clear that the route that took him past the beggar was quicker. He tried to get up early enough every morning to have time to go the long way, but now and then he ran late. When he passed the beggar, Daniel looked straight ahead as if he couldn't see the man propped against the stop sign. Sometimes, the beggar would reach out a hand to Daniel.

"Have a heart," the man would say. In a way, Daniel felt sorry for him. It made Daniel sad that the man did not have enough respect for himself to stop asking for money from strangers. But Daniel thought that if he gave the beggar money, it would only make things worse. If people would just stop giving him money, the man would see that trying to get a job was the best answer. Then maybe he'd start acting like a normal person.

One morning, Daniel woke up really late. He dressed quickly and hurried to school. At the corner, the beggar cried out to him, "I'm starving, man. Help me out a little."

Daniel started to walk away; then he turned back.

"Why don't you get a job?" he asked.

"I'm starving," the man answered.

Daniel shook his head. Well, what could he do? He didn't have any money for the guy. The next morning Daniel was late again. The beggar didn't say anything. His eyes were closed. He looked sick.

Daniel didn't walk that way again until almost a week later. He didn't see the beggar. Well, he thought, maybe that guy got it together. Then Daniel saw him lying in the gutter. The man was still alive but he looked very sick.

Daniel didn't know what to do. Maybe he should help him, but what could he do? Besides, if he didn't help him, surely someone else would. Finally, Daniel decided. He would . . .

Playing with Fire

Dear Diary,

Life is boring these days, and there's nobody around to hang out with. I haven't been to Luigi's for a pizza in a month. I haven't even seen a movie.

All I do is go to school and baby-sit. I have a new baby-sitting job for a kid who moved in next door. His name is Benjamin. He's 6, he's funny, and I like him. But he is seriously in love with fire, and yesterday I caught him lighting matches and dropping them into the leaf pile outside. Flames were shooting up, but I put them out before his parents came home.

His mother is a very nice woman, but his father is really mean. Benjamin asked me not to tell his father about the matches because, he said, his father would hit him. I could tell he was scared. His father's so mean that I'll bet he does hit him. He has a lot of money, though, and he pays me well.

I wonder sometimes if Benjamin just plays with matches to get attention. His mother seems pretty busy, and Ben's scared of his father. Every time I take the matches away, he finds some more. I'm afraid that one day he'll burn the house down, or that maybe he'll set himself on fire.

I thought about telling his mother, but I know she'll tell his father, and I don't want Benjamin to be hit. I like

Ben, and I remember what it was like to be 6. I played with matches, too, but I was one of the lucky ones who didn't burn up anything or anyone. I guess the only thing I can do is . . .

IIIIᗰ THINKING ABOUT THE STORIES

Every day, we face moral choices. We decide to cheat—or not to. We decide whether to tell the truth when it might hurt someone. We make choices that are sometimes based on the selfish desire not to get caught or because we want to look better to someone else. When you think about it, you probably make a great many moral choices.

In these stories, the characters also have to make decisions about how they're going to resolve a situation—and how they are going to live their lives. Think of some moral choices you have made and how you came to make them. Then answer the following questions.

1. Write three adjectives that describe Tracey in "Loyalties."

2. Are there any solutions to Tracey's problem that she doesn't mention in "Loyalties"? Explain.

3. What do you think Lewis is feeling when he confronts Mr. Gann in "The Choice"?

4. If you were Lewis, how would you justify turning in Mr. Gann in "The Choice"? How would you justify letting him go?

5. Write a sentence that explains the choice that Kyle faces in "Rush Hour."

6. Think about what you learned about Kyle in "Rush Hour." Then describe him.

7. If you were Lee in "The Invitation," how would you justify staying at the party? How would you justify leaving?

8. In "The Invitation," do you think Lee might be able to keep his friendship with Brad and still see Nikki? Explain.

9. Underground Z in "One Day Long Ago" faces the choice of helping his band survive and remaining true to himself. Which do you think is more important, and why?

10. What do the other band members in "One Day Long Ago" think about Underground Z? How do you know?

11. The writer in "The Secret" faces a choice between responsibility to her family and responsibility to those on the ride. Which do you think is more important, and why?

12. In "The Third Street Beggar," do Daniel's feelings about the beggar change as he sees him more often? Explain.

13. How does the situation Daniel faces in "The Third Street Beggar" differ from the situation that Kyle faces in "Rush Hour"? How is it similar?

14. Why do you think that the writer in "Playing with Fire" identifies with Benjamin?

15. How could the writer solve the problem in "Playing with Fire" without telling Benjamin's father?

Think about the moral choices that the characters must make at the end of these stories. What would you do in a similar situation? Do you think the character in the story would make the same choice?

Write an ending to one of these stories, making sure to include the results of the decision the character makes. In your ending, describe how the others in the story react to the choice.

*T*he Watcher

Finally, Roberta could relax. She got the pillow out of the old wooden box and put it against the tree. She got out her book. She put her head back, closed her eyes, and sighed. It was heaven. There was no one to tell her what to do. No one to yell at her.

There wasn't much peace in her everyday life. There was her mother screaming at her to stop daydreaming and make dinner. There was the constant sound of traffic and blaring radios on the street in front of their apartment.

Then she'd found this place. It was over the ridge by the river, where the unused railroad tracks were. It was a jungle down here. Abandoned cars and trash littered the ground. Among all the junk, though, there were beautiful old trees and flowers and wild strawberries. Peace.

She'd found an old oak whose branches made a kind of roof. Underneath was a mossy floor. She'd sat there for about an hour. After that, she'd begun to bring things there. She'd brought a box, a pillow, books, a ground cloth, a diary, and a pencil.

Roberta got out the diary and opened it. When she saw what was inside, though, her eyes widened. Someone else had made an entry.

"Pretty girl," someone had written. "Pretty, pretty girl. I'd like to get to know you. I know this seems strange, but I've been watching you. You're as pretty as the flowers around you." Roberta shut the book, her hands shaking. Suddenly, she was scared. Was someone watching her? I was positive I was alone, she said to herself. Something rustled. Frantic, Roberta got up and ran.

She didn't go back for two weeks, but she thought about the place constantly. She longed for the peace she found there. She missed the softness of the moss on her cheek and the smell of the flowers. This is stupid, she told herself. Nobody's going to chase me away.

After school that day, she went over the ridge and down to the oak tree. It was such a relief to be there, to hear the light sound of the leaves touching one another. It felt good to see her box and the mossy place where she read and slept and dreamed.

As she opened the box and took out the notebook, though, her hands were trembling.

There was another entry.

"Pretty girl, why do you run away? I want to get to know you. I won't hurt you. I could never hurt you. Please don't be frightened. Come and meet me on Saturday the 13th, here, at noon. I'll bring lunch. Please come." Roberta dropped the notebook. She shivered. It was so creepy to write in someone else's diary. Someone obviously was hiding and watching her. Shaking, she gathered her things and left.

As Saturday the 13th drew nearer, Roberta felt her thoughts drifting to the person who'd written the entries. She knew better than to go meet some guy in a lonely spot in the woods. But the diary entries were written by someone who sounded kind and nice. How could a creep write those things?

Then Saturday was here. If Roberta was going to go, she had to leave. Maybe it wasn't such a big risk. Roberta wrestled with her thoughts. Then she . . .

*F*oul Shots

Jackson couldn't sleep. He lay in his bed and thought about all the money he owed. He even owed his little sister five dollars. He didn't have a job or any hope of finding one.

At about 3 A.M., he had a brilliant idea. Maybe he could convince the people he owed to shoot foul shots with him. Jackson had heard of guys who paid off all their debts that way. He knew he could shoot foul shots better than anyone in the city.

The next day after school, the schoolyard was packed. He joined a game and played for an hour. By 5:00, four people had asked when he was going to pay them back.

"Soon," Jackson said.

"Make it sooner," they told him.

At 6:00, he announced, "I'll take on anybody for $10 a shot."

"How about right now?" a voice behind him asked. Jackson swung around and faced a tall man of about 30.

"Right this very minute?" Jackson asked.

The man nodded his head slowly. "Ten dollars a shot."

Jackson knew he was the best, but was he as good as this man? Ten perfect foul shots would get him out of debt.

"I'm ready," he said finally.

Jackson took the first shot and watched happily as it skimmed the rim and slipped through the net.

But the man's shot was perfect, and Jackson's next shot missed completely. He didn't know how it happened, but it did. Maybe he was more nervous than he thought.

The man's next shot was perfect, too. Jackson missed the next one and the one after that. The crowd couldn't believe it. Most had never seen him miss before.

"You'd better cool it," Frank whispered when Jackson came over for some water. "You're down $40."

"I can't cool it because I haven't got $40. I'll never have $40 in my entire life at this rate."

"What's the matter with you?" Frank asked. "You're good enough to go pro."

"I'm scared, man, and every single time the ball goes haywire, I get even more scared," Jackson replied.

Jackson kept it up until he was $100 down. Then the man asked, "Want to give it up?"

Jackson decided he had to keep shooting.

"Double or nothing?" the man suggested. "Look, you owe me $100 right now, and from what I hear, you don't have $100. You don't even have $5, but I'll give you a way out. If you sink your next shot, I'll forget the $100. But if you miss it, I'll want the $200 by tomorrow. What do you say?"

Jackson felt sick. His hands were shaking crazily. Where was he going to get $100? He'd have trouble finding 10 people who would give him $10 each.

"I'm waiting for your answer," the man announced. Jackson looked up at the basket and said . . .

A Long Way Down

Pete woke up earlier than usual, put on his skates, and headed for the park. It had taken a long time, but the city had finally cleared a place for in-line skaters. Now he could practice turning and skating backward. He could even wear his headphones and dance.

The park was empty, and Pete skated in a circle for a while. Then he skated backward.

By 9:00, there were five kids behind him. He knew every one of them. They didn't like him, and he didn't particularly like them.

"You think you're terrific," one of them said.

"Maybe," Pete muttered.

"How good are you really?" another kid asked.

"I'm the greatest. I can skate anywhere," said Pete.

The others laughed and asked, "Anywhere?"

"Anywhere," Pete boasted. Suddenly, he had the feeling he'd made a big mistake.

"OK," the biggest kid responded. He was older than Pete and he was really tough. "How about Captain's Hill?"

Pete knew Captain's Hill. It was the steepest hill in town.

"Captain's Hill is no problem at all," Pete said.

They stared at him, and laughed loudly. The biggest kid asked, "How about 5:00 tomorrow?"

Pete felt almost ill as he thought about the cars on Captain's Hill. The traffic at 5:00 would be wicked, and the commuters would be speeding down the hill at 60 miles an hour. It would be the toughest thing he'd ever done, but he wanted to do it. He'd be famous if he made it down alive.

"I'll be there," Pete announced.

Yet, Pete was terrified because the hill was too steep. There was no way to stop. He'd have to skate all the way down before he stopped, and there was a highway at the bottom. He wouldn't be able to stop before he crossed it, so all he could do was hope the light at the bottom would be green when he got there.

That night, he didn't sleep. He kept thinking about the hill and the light at the bottom. What would he do if it were red? He wouldn't be able to stop. He'd be a dead man.

But he still wanted to do it because the whole school would be talking about him. People would look at him when he walked down the street.

Everyone was waiting when he arrived at 5:00. There must have been 50 kids there. He skated to the top of the hill and looked down at the light at the bottom. He was surprised that he could see it and regretted that he hadn't timed it the day before.

Traffic was extremely heavy, and it was moving very fast. This is crazy, Pete thought. I might make it through the cars, but I'll die if the light is red.

He glanced around and saw that everyone was waiting for him to go. In a second, the guy was going to blow the whistle signaling him to start.

Suddenly, the shrill sound of the whistle rang in his ears. He made his decision and . . .

Elisha's Dog

Elisha looked over her shoulder to see if the collie mutt was still there. The dog looked up at her with those smart dog eyes and seemed to smile. Elisha turned back around. Every time she looked at that face she felt like crying. There was no way she could walk into her house with a dog. Especially not a dirty, ragged dog like the one that was following her. Her dad would never go for it. Her dad wasn't a bad guy. He just had a mean temper, and he didn't like animals. Elisha knew the rules.

She could hear the dog panting behind her. Considering how thin it was, it was probably starving. She spotted a convenience store across the street. That was it. She'd go into the store and get the dog some water, and if the mutt was still there when she came out, then she'd have to decide what to do. The dog trotted after her.

"See ya," she whispered, half hopefully.

Inside, she asked the man behind the counter for a cup of water. Next to the soda cooler sat little bags of dog food. Should she get one? She went to the window and looked out. The dog sat patiently beside a fire hydrant. Oh, how Elisha wanted to take that dog home. She would feed him, give him a bath, and let him sleep at the foot of her bed. He could walk with her to school in the mornings and be there, waiting, when she got out. Maybe the dog was thinking the same things. Elisha knew he was waiting for her. She looked at the bag of dog food.

"I'll take this, too," she told the cashier.

The mutt lapped at the water until it was gone and even for a little while after that. Elisha opened the bag of food and poured a little onto the ground.

"All right, now. You can't follow me anymore," she said. "I've done what I can. You can have the rest of this food, but you have to stay here. You can't come with me."

Elisha rose and began to walk away. She looked back. The dog still sat there, eating. She kept walking. It wasn't until she was at the corner near her house that she heard clicking behind her. It was the kind of clicking sound a dog's feet make on the pavement. Elisha looked behind her. The dog wagged its tail. Elisha had no idea what to do. Finally, she decided that she would . . .

Just My Luck

J.L. held out his ticket and waited for the ticket taker to rip it in half. When he did, J.L. flipped the stub aside and pushed his way to his seat.

Boy, was he lucky! The concert had been sold out for months, but then his friend Ace had gotten sick and sold J.L. his ticket. J.L. fell into his seat and thought, This is amazing! In 15 minutes I'm going to hear my favorite band.

The band started to play at 8:00. They performed their biggest hit first. J.L. shoved his way into the aisle, raised his arms, and let the music take him away.

When the concert was over, J.L. walked slowly to the train. He was glad he had a two-hour ride home. He could replay the concert in his mind and listen to his tape on the train. He couldn't wait to play the band's hit song over and over.

J.L. took a seat at the back of the car and slipped on his headphones as the train pulled slowly out of the station. After a while, a man tapped his shoulder, but J.L. didn't notice. The man tapped him again, and this time J.L. looked up. The conductor wanted his ticket, so he dug into his pocket and handed it to him. The conductor took it and punched it. J.L. tossed it across the aisle.

The following morning, J.L. was awakened early by a loud knock on his apartment door. Two policemen entered. One of them mumbled, "You're in trouble, kid."

J.L. didn't say anything. He couldn't believe what he was hearing. He searched his brain, trying to remember if he had done anything wrong.

"Where were you yesterday?" the second policeman asked.

"When?" asked J.L.

"Around 7:00 P.M."

J.L. asked if he was being accused of something. The policeman shrugged. "Somebody stole a lot of TVs from a store on Hanover Street last night. We thought you might know something about it," he said.

J.L. knew he was under suspicion because he had been in trouble before. Would he never be able to put that behind him?

"I was at a concert," he insisted. "I wasn't even around."

"Can you prove it?" the policeman asked.

J.L. didn't know if he could prove it or not. He thought for a long moment and then answered . . .

On the Road

Sly rode his bike over to Peter's house and knocked on the door. "Ready? he asked as Peter was opening the door.

"Ready for what?" Peter answered.

Sly laughed out loud and said, "Your new life, man. Are you ready for your exciting new life? Are you ready to come with me? Decide. In two days, I'll be gone."

Sly pulled a bus ticket out of his pocket and waved it above his head. "I can go anywhere with this ticket," he shouted. "I can explore everywhere in the United States of America. Come with me, Peter."

Peter smiled and shook his head. He couldn't go. In six months he would be finished with high school, and in the fall he would start college. Before long, he would be able to help kids who were abused by their parents.

"Not now, Sly," he said.

Sly shrugged and walked toward the door. "I'll call you tomorrow in case you change your mind."

Peter's father staggered in drunk again that night. It was the third night in a row. Peter lay on his bed and listened. Soon, his father would start to throw things, and then he'd begin to swing his fists around. If his mother wasn't careful, she would feel those fists.

Peter pulled the covers over his head and tried not to listen. He knew that his mother would be really quiet. She had learned to keep out of her husband's way.

Why doesn't she leave him, Peter wondered. He had been wondering that all his life. Why hadn't she taken Peter away when he was little? Why shouldn't he leave with Sly in two days? Was it really because he wanted to finish school and help other abused kids, or was it because he was afraid to leave his mother? Or was he simply afraid?

Peter's father didn't hit anyone that night, and he didn't break any dishes or furniture. He just passed out.

The next morning, Peter called Sly and said, "When are you leaving?"

"Tomorrow morning," Sly replied.

"What time?" Peter asked.

"I'm taking the 2:00 bus to Chicago. Why?"

"I don't know," Peter said. "I might come."

"All right! You're going to forget about school?" Sly asked.

"I don't know," Peter said again. "I just don't know." But deep in his heart he did know. He took a deep breath and said to Sly . . .

An unexpected situation occurs, and suddenly you're facing trouble—or worse. You have to think on your feet to try to make a decision. If you make the wrong one, you could be facing a bigger problem. That's what this unit is all about. The characters have to make a choice—and usually, they've put themselves in the difficult position. How will she decide if the possible downside of a risk is worth the possible gain? Will he ignore the danger and keep his pride? Will she take a risk and end up in more trouble?

The characters in this unit have to deal with situations in which a bad decision could lead to big trouble. Try to put yourself in these characters' shoes. What would you do? How would you make a decision? Use your experience and that of your friends to help you answer the questions below.

1. What risks does Roberta face in "The Watcher" if she decides to return to meet the writer?

2. Describe Roberta in "The Watcher," based on what you learned about her in the story.

3. What reasons might there be for Jackson to be so nervous as he plays the tall man in "Foul Shots"?

4. In "Foul Shots," which do you think is the bigger risk, shooting the double-or-nothing shot or trying to find the money to pay the tall man? Explain.

5. How are Pete in "A Long Way Down" and Jackson in "Foul Shots" similar? How do you think these traits will influence their decisions?

6. Do you think Pete in "A Long Way Down" is sorry that he took the dare to blade down Captain's Hill? Give examples from the story that justify your answer.

7. What is the risk if Elisha in "Elisha's Dog" takes the dog home? Is there another way for her to solve her problem?

8. In "Elisha's Dog," what kind of relationship do you think Elisha and her father have? How will this relationship affect what Elisha does?

9. Write two possible ways that J.L. in "Just My Luck" could prove he was not the TV thief.

10. Write three adjectives that describe J.L. in "Just My Luck." How will J.L.'s personality affect how he deals with the policeman?

11. What kinds of consequences will Peter face if he decides to leave with Sly in "On the Road"?

12. Why do you think Peter in "On the Road" is interested in a career helping abused kids? Do you think he might really be able to help them? Explain.

IIIII THINKING ABOUT THE ENDING

The characters in the stories in this unit face painful choices. In some cases, they are choosing between safety and physical harm. Think about the stories, and choose one you would like to finish. How does the character get through the situation? Does the character's decision make his or her life more or less difficult?

Write an ending to the story in which you chart a course of action for the character. Keep in mind the character you're writing the ending for. What would this character do, based on what you have learned about him or her in the story? Write in your ending how the character makes his or her decision and what the results are.

In Line with Sandy Koufax

Michael felt the sting of catching the ball. Suddenly, his whole team was yelling and running toward him.

"You did it again, Michael!"

"We won! We won!" they cried. Michael felt himself being raised into the air. The thrill of being lifted up like that, not knowing if a few hands would let go and he would go tumbling, was almost like the thrill of baseball itself.

One thing Michael loved about baseball was the uncertainty. Another thing was that working hard could mean the difference between winning and losing.

After the game, Michael showered and changed for Friday dinner. Michael loved Friday nights at home. His mother would say a prayer over the candles. His sister would say the prayer for bread. At dinner, his father would explain points of Jewish law, and his mother would tell stories of the history of the Jews.

Saturday was a good day at Michael's house. It was holy. No one could use electricity or talk on the phone. The laws were to make sure no work was done on the Sabbath.

After the game, everyone agreed that the team was good enough to join the county league. Michael was chosen to be the team's pitcher. He couldn't stop smiling as he walked home from the game. Then he stopped suddenly. There was a problem—a big problem. Because most of the kids went to church on Sunday, the county league's games were played on Saturday. Playing baseball on the Sabbath would mean breaking Jewish law. He didn't want to break the law, but if he wasn't on the team, then he'd never get to play.

"Have you heard of Sandy Koufax?" his father asked.

"Of course, Dad. He was the best pitcher in—"

Michael's father smiled and continued, "Have you ever heard what he did when his team went to the World Series and he was going to have to pitch on Yom Kippur, the holiest day of the Jewish year?"

"He didn't pitch?" Michael asked.

"He didn't pitch," answered his father.

Michael didn't know what to do. He was no Sandy Koufax, and this was no World Series, but he wanted to play ball. His father hadn't helped him at all. He'd only made the choice more difficult.

The morning of the game, Michael stood staring at his playing clothes. After a long time, he decided. He would . . .

Big Mama's Letter

October 11, 1965

To my family,

Few people get to live as long as I have—112 years. That's the reason, of course, that those reporters came to interview me today about slavery and change. I told them that some things had changed for the better but that other things had gotten worse. Then I looked across the room at all of you, my sons and your children and grandchildren. You were there because the reporter invited you to join the interview. It was your first visit in months.

By now, most of you are doctors, lawyers, teachers, and businesspeople. You've all finished college or trade school and made good lives for yourselves. I'm proud of that. But just before the reporters showed up, you said something that bothered me.

You tried convincing me to move from my house. You want to pay for me to live in an old folks' home in some fancy neighborhood. As you know, I refused. As soon as the reporters left, I chased you all away. I said that if you really care, you'll come by more often and visit. Closing the door nearly broke my heart. But I needed you to know how I felt. In an old folks' home, surrounded by strangers, I'd be lonely for sure. Here, my neighbors treat me like family.

I've been in this house since the start of the century. Over my fireplace, I have the cowbells that were locked to my ankles and wrists. My master put them on me so that he could hear where I went. There's also a rusty key, given to me by my master's daughter, who felt sorry for me.

The man who owned me was Donald Butterness, but we called him Master Bitterness. It seemed he was always thinking up new ways of keeping me from running off. Runaways were a problem for all slave owners. But no matter how often I was beaten, I kept running away. After the Civil War freed us, I swore I would spend my life in freedom. A nursing home would take that away from me. I hope you understand. I love you all.

With love,
Big Mama

Dear Big Mama,

I'm sorry it has taken so long for me to write. As the writer in the family, I was chosen by the others to answer your letter. Well, I've been very busy—I'm teaching a class at Howard University this winter, writing another book, and always driving the girls here and there. Life is full.

It was hard for us, too, that day when you told us never to come back. I know we should visit you more. But as you know, we're all so busy. The drive takes hours.

Not only would you be safer in the nursing home, but also you'd be closer to us. We'd be able to visit you more often. Erica was just saying that she'd like to interview you for her class history project. That would be wonderful, wouldn't it?

I hope you'll write back and tell me whether you're willing to make this sacrifice so that your great-great-grandchildren have a chance to get to know you.

With affection, your great-granddaughter,
Ursula

November 15, 1965

Dear Ursula,

I've reread your letter several times and have given the matter much thought. Here is what I've decided . . .

Promised Land

"Anything to declare?" asked the customs inspector.
"What did he say?" the boy asked in Pilipino.
"He wants to know if we have something to declare," his older sister Carmen translated.

"What does that mean?" Carmen's brother asked.

"I don't know," she admitted.

The room was crowded with people who had been on their plane. They were waiting in line to get into the United States.

"Anything to declare?" the man asked again.

"I have something to declare," Father said.

Oh no, Carmen thought. Father had the face he always made when he was about to give a speech.

"I am declaring that I am a new man," he told the inspector. "We are here to start a new life!"

"Yeah, that's nice," the inspector said flatly.

Carmen couldn't believe she was here. Only yesterday, they were in the Philippines. Father had promised them a new life in America. He had stopped drinking. He had gotten back together with Mother and even persuaded her to come with them. Carmen was surprised that she did.

Carmen and her brother stood and watched Father make a speech to the inspector. They watched the man open their boxes and bags.

They left customs an hour later. Carmen and her brother walked with their mother. Father walked ahead of them. He pretended to know where he was going.

Carmen looked at her mother. "What are you thinking, Ma?" she asked.

"I'm thinking about many things," she replied.

"I'm happy you're back with us," Carmen told her.

Mother looked at her. She didn't seem as happy as Carmen was. "Now that we're here in America," Mother whispered, "I have to tell you something. You know I love you and your brother very much."

"Yes, Ma. I know."

"That's why I came with you to America," Mother explained. "I needed you to get me in."

"I know." Carmen nodded.

"It's hard for me to tell you this," Mother continued, starting to cry. "Now that we are here in America, I am going to divorce your father."

"Divorce!" Carmen gasped. "That's a sin!"

"Not in the United States," Mother whispered.

Carmen remembered how the priest used to say bad things about people who were divorced.

"Have you told Father?" Carmen asked.

"No, not yet. It's our secret," Mother answered.

"Come on!" Father yelled. He had his directions.

They walked quickly to catch up with the men. Carmen's brother tugged at her. "Why is Ma crying?"

Carmen didn't speak. She wanted to cry, too.

"What's wrong with you women?" Father barked.

Carmen looked at her father, then at her mother. Her brother was waiting for an answer.

Finally, she said . . .

Warrior Week

The August air smelled like autumn in Browning, Montana. A smoky haze blown in by a breeze from the canyons hung over the little reservation town. Tom Longhair wondered why he had given in and agreed to run cross-country. Historically, Native Americans have excelled at long-distance running, and Tom's father had been a successful collegiate runner. Now everyone expected Tom to be the next Longhair runner.

He bent over to check his shoelaces before he began what the kids called Warrior Week. It would be a grueling seven days. Some runners would drop out.

The elders approached running seriously. They prayed for healthy, strong runners. Tom's dad must have explained it to him a hundred times: "It's one of the ways that the Blackfeet Nation holds on to our past glory. Blackfeet runners are tall, strong, and sleek. When our families go to meets around the state, we look good and feel good." In a quiet voice he would always add, "We get respect."

Tom knew what his father was talking about. There was only one problem. He didn't want to run.

Tom slowly approached the rest of the team, waiting outside the gym for the coach. They were all smiling. That is, everyone was smiling but the freshmen.

It's no big deal, Tom thought. I'll just keep running, no matter what. He had just started to stretch when Coach Weston approached.

"Hop into the back of the pick-ups," the coach said with a smile. "We're going to take you out a ways just to get you started today."

The boys' team hopped into the back of three pick-ups. One after another, the trucks pulled out onto the county road. After a few miles, they pulled off the main road and turned down a dirt cow trail heading toward the foothills. Finally, they pulled to a stop.

"Hop out," the coach wheezed. "Have a nice run home, boys."

The boys started at a slow jog. No one seemed in a big hurry to beat the others.

For the first mile, Tom thought of all the reasons he was going to give for quitting when he got home. After about two miles, he began to notice the rest of the team. Everyone was having a good time. Just about the time you felt like your lungs would burn a hole right through your chest, someone would tell you how ridiculous you looked and the team would laugh. Even Tom laughed.

When it was over, the team had run 10 miles. As he dragged himself into the showers, Tom thought about the team. Everyone was tired, but no one had quit. He felt something new—a kind of self-honor. Tom felt good. But could he keep it up every day for a week?

Leaving the gym, he noticed his dad standing beside their old Ford truck. Tom hopped in, not yet ready to talk about cross-country. The ride home was a little awkward. Usually they were free with one another, but tonight Tom and his dad both kept a quiet distance, as each waited for the other to raise the subject.

Dinner wasn't much different—the family was quiet. Gulping his food, Tom kept his eyes on his plate. It was his younger brother Lewis who just had to ask, "So are you going to do it? Are you going to run?" Tom looked at his brother and replied . . .

Music Lesson

"Cool drum solo!"

"Yeah, your tablet was cool."

"It's called a tabla," Bavan told his listeners. Ignorant Americans, he thought. Why had he agreed to play in the school talent show? To them, he was just banging on a drum. They didn't understand the spirit of Indian music.

Bavan carefully picked up his tabla. He remembered what his parents had said ever since they left India: Americans don't understand. They're right, he thought.

Bavan walked into the crowded hallway. He held his tabla tightly. He didn't want it to get bumped.

"Excuse me," he said, dodging left and right.

"Cool music!" someone yelled.

"Thank you," he muttered.

Bavan turned the corner. He made his way to the principal's office. They would let him leave his tabla there. He didn't want to risk breaking it.

"Excellent performance, Bavan," the school secretary told him. He put his tabla down by her desk. "I love Indian music. I'm very impressed."

"Thank you," Bavan said. He wondered if she was just being polite. Bavan headed for his locker.

"I enjoyed your playing, Bavan," he heard.

Bavan turned around. There stood Jennifer. She's pretty, he thought, for an American.

Jennifer embarrassed Bavan. He had known her since elementary school. She was smart and polite. Jennifer was the only American who understood him. He could talk to her. She was his only American friend.

Secretly, he wanted her to be more than a friend. He could not understand his feelings lately. Jennifer seemed prettier than before.

His parents had warned him about Americans. They were greedy, selfish, and ignorant. It seemed true. Everybody at school was rude and dumb. They made fun of him. But Jennifer was different. She was interested in him. She made Bavan feel good, but uneasy.

"I'd love to hear you play more," Jennifer told him. "I felt there was something very special in your music."

"Really?" Bavan asked. He was surprised to hear an American say that.

"Yes," she said. "It carried me away."

"Well," Bavan said, "I don't normally give concerts."

"I wish you would. At least for me," she responded. "Would you play for me at your house?"

"Uhmm . . . " He didn't know if it would be proper. His parents didn't like having Americans in their house.

"Well?" she asked. "May I?"

Bavan didn't know what to say. He looked down at his feet. His heart was beating fast. It was the same feeling he had when he played the tabla. He wanted her to come to his house. He wanted to play for her.

If she weren't American, I'd ask her out, he thought. He didn't know what to say.

"If you don't want me to," Jennifer said, "I won't."

"Oh, no, that's not it," he said.

"Well, what is it then?" she asked.

Bavan took a deep breath. Then he said . . .

Most families have traditions, from something as simple as holiday dinners to religious beliefs that prevent them from eating certain foods. When people within families decide to ignore or change traditions, confusion is sometimes the result. At other times, family members feel angry, threatened, and betrayed. The characters in these stories face decisions about how to live their lives. They have to decide whether to live as they want and what the result of that decision might mean for everyone in their family. Tradition in these stories can be a comfort to the main characters. It can also keep them from doing what they really want to do.

As you answer these questions, try to put yourself in the shoes of the characters facing the question: Should I break with tradition or not?

1. How important is tradition to Michael's family in "In Line with Sandy Koufax"? How can you tell?

2. How do you think Michael's parents would feel if he decided to join the team in "In Line with Sandy Koufax"? Give evidence from the story to explain your answer.

3. Give one argument for Big Mama in "Big Mama's Letter" to remain at her home and one argument for her to move.

4. What can you tell about Ursula from the letter she writes to Big Mama in "Big Mama's Letter"?

5. Describe the relationship between the family members in "Promised Land."

6. How does moving to the United States give the mother in "Promised Land" the chance to break with tradition?

7. Why is Tom hesitating about quitting the team in "Warrior Week"?

8. How do you think Tom's father would feel about his breaking with tradition in "Warrior Week"? Use examples from the story to explain your answer.

9. Explain the similarity in the situation Bavan faces in "Music Lesson" and the situation Tom faces in "Warrior Week."

10. Why do you think Bavan's parents don't want Americans in their home?

IIIII THINKING ABOUT THE ENDING

Cultural differences and traditions are important in this unit. Parents and children have misunderstandings and different expectations of one another. Often, these problems are based on the parents being more firmly attached to another culture, while their children want to become more American. Sometimes the children, too, feel tied to their culture and must decide how to balance the demands of living in two cultures.

Choose a story whose characters interest you. Then write an ending for that story, keeping in mind the cultural differences the main character faces. Is there another way for the character to resolve the problem that might not have been mentioned in the story? Include in your ending the effects the decision has on all of the characters in the story.

The Boy in the Mall

It was Saturday afternoon. Rick and Shauna were heading slowly toward Pepperoni Pete's for a pizza.

"Uh-oh," Rick said. "Screaming kid alert."

Shauna heard a wailing toddler and groaned. She had enough of that at home from her little sister Torrie.

The crying grew louder. Then they saw the toddler, a little boy about 2 years old, walking between two teenaged boys, who were holding both his hands. The older boys were in a hurry, pulling the little one along so fast that his chubby legs could hardly keep up.

As they walked past, Rick said in a low voice, "Aren't they being kind of rough with him?"

"Yeah," Shauna agreed, "but they're no worse than a lot of parents I've seen. Besides, that kid probably did something awful. Why do people take little kids shopping?"

Rick frowned. "I think something's going on. Maybe they're kidnapping him."

"Kidnapping? In broad daylight? Come on, Rick," Shauna said.

Rick insisted, "I think we ought to check this out. Let's double back."

"Rick . . ."

84

"Come on! They're walking fast. We've got to hurry!" Rick grabbed her hand, turned around, and began to run.

They ran to the top of the escalator. There were the boys, with the crying toddler between them. Shauna saw Rick give them a hard stare.

Rick said, "Did you see the way other people are looking at them? They think something's wrong, too. Neither one of them looks like the little guy's brother."

"Lots of brothers and sisters don't look alike," Shauna replied. "I can't believe they're kidnapping him. I mean, I know things like that happen, but . . . " She shook her head. It was too weird to imagine a kidnapping here, in the mall she'd been coming to since she was 7.

"I think we ought to tell a cop," Rick told her.

"Rick, what would you say? What makes you think a cop's going to believe you?" Shauna asked.

"Let's find out," Rick said. "There ought to be a cop around here somewhere."

"Oh, Rick, come on," Shauna said. "Are you sure that little boy's being kidnapped?"

"No, I am not sure," Rick answered.

"Then forget it. You don't want to look like an idiot, do you? Let's go get some pizza," Shauna said.

Rick looked at her and said . . .

Helping Hand

Raquel looked around her mom's bedroom at all the new clothes that lay folded on the bed. "This is a lot of stuff!" she cried.

This is pretty, she thought, picking up a sweater. It was soft and warm. Raquel carefully unfolded the sweater. She held it up and looked in the mirror. If I were a little bigger, she thought, this would look nice on me.

She looked at the brand. Its name sounded expensive. She tried to find a price tag. All she could find was a big piece of plastic stuck to the sleeve. Raquel wondered how to remove it without ripping the sweater.

Ever since her mom had gotten a new job near the mall, she came home with nice things almost every day. Raquel worried that her mom might be spending too much money. If she saved some of it, they could move out of their small apartment.

Raquel decided that she would help her mother save. They had been learning things in math class about shopping. If she went with her mother, she could help her save by looking for bargains. But Mom never let Raquel come with her to the mall.

Raquel decided to look in the bags for the receipts. She wanted to add them up and see how much all the clothes were worth. But Raquel couldn't find one receipt. Just then her mom came in.

"What are you doing, Raquel?" she asked.

"I'm looking at the new clothes you bought," Raquel said.

"Aren't they nice?" said her mother.

"Yes. They must have been expensive."

Raquel's mom didn't answer her. She walked over to the bed and started to sort through her new clothes.

"Tomorrow, I'll get you a new dress," her mom said.

Raquel smiled. It would be nice to have a new dress. But she thought about saving money. "That's OK, Mom," she said. "I think we should save some of our money. Where are the receipts for all this stuff?"

Her mother turned and looked at her. "Why?" she asked.

"I know a lot of math from school," said Raquel. "They taught us how to add and save."

"That's nice, but it doesn't matter."

Raquel was a little annoyed with her mother. "You might be spending too much," she said.

Mom continued sorting her new clothes. "I have a special five-finger discount," she laughed.

Raquel had heard that phrase before. The kids who lived downstairs used to say it all the time whenever they came back from the candy store with their pockets full of candy. Later, she realized that they had been stealing.

"What's your size now?" her mom asked again.

"Why?" Raquel asked.

"If I'm going to get you a new dress, I need to know."

Raquel didn't want a new dress or anything else if her mom was stealing. Maybe she was only joking.

"Why don't I just come with you?" Rachel suggested.

"No," said her mother. "You're not allowed."

Raquel was worried. Why wasn't she allowed, she thought. Raquel looked at all the nice new clothes. She thought about the boys stealing candy. She looked up at her mother and said . . .

Team Spirit

When the final bell rang, Max raced to the board. "Yes!" he cried. "I'm the first and only freshman in the history of this school to make the varsity wrestling team."

Max couldn't wait to get home and tell his family. They would all be as excited as he was. They had come to every one of his matches in middle school.

Max made his announcement after the family was settled around the dinner table. He filled his plate with salad and skipped the rest.

"Aren't you hungry?" his mother asked.

"Got to watch the weight," he replied. "I made the team."

Max's father jumped up so fast his chair turned over. "I knew you could do it!" he cried.

"Wait'll I tell your aunts and uncles!" his mother shouted.

"No more junk food, Mom," Max said.

"Of course not," his mother replied. "We've got to keep you in top shape."

Max watched his diet carefully for the next few weeks. He ate fruit, vegetables, bread, and a little chicken. He ran five miles a day and lifted weights. He was in fine shape.

"You're looking extremely good these days," his sister said. "Tell me your secret."

"No secret," Max told her. "My body is my temple." He was a vision of good health.

"We've got a tough match next week," the coach announced. "This team is the best in the city. I'm going to put it bluntly. I suspect they're taking steroids. I think we should fight fire with fire."

"What does that mean?" Max whispered to his team-mate.

"It means that he wants us to take steroids," the other boy said.

"No way!" Max said aloud. "I'm not taking steroids—or any other drug."

"Why not, Max?" the coach asked.

"Because I don't want to harm my body. Anyway, what if we got caught? My parents would be furious."

"From what I hear," the coach said, "your parents are delighted that you're on the team. I think they'd be angrier if you weren't on the team, Max."

Max knew he had to choose: Take steroids or be thrown off the team.

That night at dinner, Max ate gravy, cake, fries, and anything else he could stuff into his mouth. His family watched him, puzzled.

"How's the wrestling?" his mother asked. "We're so proud of you, Max."

"Maybe I won't wrestle," Max muttered.

"But you have to, Max," his father said sternly. "Your aunts and uncles and Grandma and Grandpa are coming."

Max's head was spinning. He didn't want to disappoint his family. He wanted to be on the team. But he didn't want to take any kind of drug. Suddenly, he made his decision. He would . . .

Managing

Bethany walked quickly from the college to the corner bus stop. She hurried because she didn't want to be late for work at Joseph's Restaurant. Bethany tried never to be late for work, but these days it was especially important. The night manager had quit a week ago, and Joseph, the owner, was looking for a new manager.

As the bus brought her closer to the restaurant, Bethany thought about how much better things would be if she were the night manager of Joseph's. She could start to pay for college herself. Her dad had already told her he couldn't give her any more money. He was glad that she was taking classes in restaurant management. They both hoped that someday Bethany would have her own restaurant. When that day came, Bethany promised herself she would pay her dad back every cent he'd given her, plus a lot more. But for now, the important thing was to get this manager's job. It could be her first step up that ladder.

As Bethany cut lettuce for salads in the back kitchen, Joseph came up to her.

"Hey, Beth," he said. "Could you manage the restaurant tonight? I have to go home because my kid is sick. Would you mind?"

"I'd be happy to, Joseph. Don't worry about it."

"Thanks, Beth. Look, this is what you have to do—"

"Joseph," Bethany interrupted, smiling. "I know what to do. Go home to your kid. I'll take care of everything."

After Joseph left, Bethany checked to make sure that everything was ready for the dinner rush. One of the waitresses stood at the bar, rolling silverware into napkins.

"Everything set, Lucy?" Bethany asked her.

"Yeah," Lucy answered without looking up. Bethany knew why Lucy wouldn't look at her. Lucy had worked at Joseph's longer than anybody. She was a single mother. Her kids had one shirt, one pair of pants, and one set of sneakers each. If Lucy got the job, her kids wouldn't have to go to school without lunch money. Maybe they could even move to a better place.

Bethany knew all this, but she also knew that Lucy probably wouldn't make a good manager. Lucy became angry too quickly. She yelled at people for little mistakes. She didn't explain things well, so she ended up making things harder.

As Bethany locked the restaurant door behind her that night, she felt a tap on her shoulder.

"Bethany," Lucy asked, "can we talk?"

"Sure," Bethany said, trying to smile.

It took Lucy a long time before she spoke again.

"Bethany, I know you want that job. You would be good at it. Joseph will give you the job if you ask for it. But I need this job more than you right now, Bethany. Please let me have a chance at it."

"But, Lucy," Bethany said slowly. "I need this job, too. My dad can't pay for my classes anymore. If I have to quit school, I'll end up . . ." like you, she almost said.

"You're young, Bethany. You'll have other chances. I've got two kids at home who don't have any winter clothes. If one of them gets sick, I can't even afford to go to the doctor. Please, Bethany."

Bethany didn't know what to say. Should she tell Lucy that the best person for the job should get it? Should she tell her she could have the job?

"Lucy," Bethany said . . .

*P*arents, Please Come Home

Tina held the phone with one hand and drummed her fingers on the couch with the other. One ring, two rings. "Please be home," she whispered.

"Hello." It was Bobby.

"Bobby, I'm so glad you're there!" Tina's voice was shaky.

"What's wrong? You sound scared," Bobby said.

"I don't know what to do, Bobby. I'm still here with the kids at the Darnell's house. The parents haven't come home yet."

"What?" said Bobby. "You were only supposed to baby-sit for the weekend! They're two days late!"

"I know," Tina said. "They said they'd be back early Sunday afternoon, but they haven't called or anything."

"Don't you have a number where you can reach them?" Bobby asked.

"No, I don't," Tina answered. "They said they were driving up to Naughton for the weekend. That's all. I don't know what we're going to do for breakfast tomorrow if they don't show up. We've eaten just about everything in the house."

"Did you tell your mom about it?" asked Bobby.

"I can't reach her," Tina asked. "Bobby, I don't know what to do!"

"I'm coming over," Bobby said.

"Okay," Tina said. "I'll leave the porch light on."

Tina turned on the light and then walked into the room where the kids were sleeping. There was Debra, age 8, sharing the bed with her 5-year-old sister Tara. In the crib was Kevin, age 3. He gave me such a hard time today, Tina thought. But now he looks sweet with his mouth open, hugging a grubby stuffed bunny. Tina whispered, "Good night, little guy."

She picked up a sock from the floor and thought, I'm all they've got right now.

When Bobby arrived, he told her, "I think we ought to call the cops."

"I don't know," Tina said. "If I do that, they might take the kids away. They could put them in foster homes."

"Maybe that should happen," said Bobby. "People who just leave their kids like this shouldn't be parents."

"But Bobby, they'd probably put each kid in a separate home. That would be awful!" Tina exclaimed. She stared at the rug, frowning. She continued, "I could borrow some money from Mom. I could buy enough food to last a couple more days. They're bound to come home soon."

"Those people went off and left their kids—that's child abuse!" Bobby said. "What are they going to do to these kids next if you don't report them?"

Tina looked at the clock. It was almost 11:00. She could call her mom and ask for money for groceries, or she could call the cops. She looked at Bobby for a long moment. Then she walked over to the phone. She announced, "I'm going to . . ."

A Different Face

Josie brought her face close to the mirror over the sink, examining her chin and then her forehead.

She ran a hand down her brown cheek, watching the girl in the mirror do the same. It reminded her of the time that she and her best friend Andrew had dressed as werewolves for Halloween, smearing the makeup on each others' cheeks and laughing. That was the one time nobody bugged us, Josie thought, because for once, our faces were the same color.

She smiled at her reflection—for all the trouble their friendship had caused, Josie felt lucky to have Andrew as a friend. Of course, things had gotten a little strained since her stepdaddy had forbidden him to come around. Josie had to sneak out if she wanted to see him. She could hear the thunk of her stepsister's footsteps in the hallway.

"I'm going out," Josie said to Onika.

"You'd better not be going to see that China-boy," Onika warned.

"What's wrong with all of you!" Josie yelled. "Black, white, yellow, or purple—what's the difference? You all yelled at me for being too shy, and now that I finally have a friend, you don't like him. And he's not Chinese, he's Korean!"

Just then, Josie heard a sharp clink against her bedroom window. Andrew was tossing pebbles at the glass to signal her. She moved down the hall past Onika, shutting her bedroom door behind her. She ran to the window and tugged it open.

"What are you doing here?" she called down to the black-haired figure on the street below. "I told you I'd meet you at the park around 4:00."

"I want to talk to you, and I couldn't wait that long," Andrew responded.

"I'll be right down," Josie whispered.

Onika's daddy, Josie's new stepdaddy, was well known in the neighborhood. He had organized neighborhood watches to help catch drug dealers. He was a good man, but he thought people should love and marry only people of their own culture. No matter how hard I try, I can't make him understand about Andrew, Josie thought.

Andrew was sitting on the steps of the old corner market. He jumped up when he saw Josie.

"Hey," she said, smiling. "what'd you do today?"

Andrew kicked at the ground with the rubber toe of his sneaker. "Thought a lot."

"What'd you think about?" she asked softly.

"It's not right for us to sneak around, Josie. How can we really be friends if we're always worried that someone's going to catch us hanging out together?"

Josie nodded. "All this lying is making me sick."

"We have to decide," Andrew said. "We stand up to your stepfather, or we stop hanging out."

Josie held her head in her hands. "Stand up to him?" Things had finally settled down a little for her and Mama—how could she shake them up again?

"I have to get home," he said. "Think about this. We'll talk tomorrow at school about what to do, OK?" He hugged her and left. Josie slowly walked home.

Her stepfather opened the front door for her. "Hi, darlin'," he greeted her. "Where've you been?"

Josie thought about all that Andrew had said. She looked up at her stepfather and answered, . . .

Big Money

Cardell Brown had been getting ready for this moment all his life. He had started to play football when he was 6 years old. His brothers taught him how to throw the ball, how to position his feet, and how to bend his elbow.

Cardell was very talented, and he knew it. In six months, he would be out of high school. Then it was college. Cardell couldn't wait.

"How are you going to pay for college?" his brothers asked him. They had gone to work after high school.

"I'll get a football scholarship," Cardell had said.

They laughed when he said that. "A football scholarship from this little town? No football scout's going to travel all the way down here," they said.

"They'll come," Cardell insisted. "They'll come to the county finals, just wait and see."

But that was several weeks ago. Now it was time for the championship game, and Cardell was worried. What if they didn't come? Then he wouldn't be able to go to college, and college was Cardell's only way out.

On the night before the game, Cardell went to bed at 8:00. He wanted to be well rested for the game. At 9:00, the phone rang. Cardell heard his mom say he was asleep.

"I'm awake, Mom," Cardell shouted. He jumped out of bed and hurried into the living room. He took the phone from his mother and said, "Hello?"

"You alone?" a man's voice muttered.

Cardell glanced around. His mother had left, so he said, "Yeah. Who's this?"

"Never mind the name. We just wanted to tell you that we're betting on the other team in tomorrow's game."

Cardell laughed and said, "Thanks for telling me. I'm delighted for you. Now may I go back to bed?"

"We have something to ask you," the man said. "We know that you need money for college."

Cardell wondered where this was going.

"How are you going to pay for college, kid?"

"I'll get a scholarship when the scouts come down to see me tomorrow," Cardell explained.

"Let's suppose that they don't come," the man said.

"They'll come," Cardell insisted quickly.

"I have an idea," the man said. "We're betting big bucks on the other team, and we want them to win. If you play badly, the other team will win. Do you understand?"

"I understand extremely well, but I am not going to play badly," Cardell said. "I'm going to play well because the scouts will be there."

"They aren't coming," the man told him. "Maybe we've arranged it so they won't be there, and if that's so, you won't go to college unless you take our offer."

"What offer?" asked Cardell.

"We'll pay your college tuition if you'll just throw this game."

"You're joking, and anyway, they'll come," Cardell said. But he wasn't so sure.

"I'm telling you. This is the deal. Think about it. I'll call you in an hour," the man said.

Cardell spent the next hour thinking, and when the phone rang, he was ready. He'd decided to . . .

Treasure

The boys were looking everywhere for the fat white cat.
"Here, kitty, kitty, kitty," Jimmy called. He turned to his brother.
"I feel like an idiot, searching for a stupid cat."

"Well, you let her out," said Kit. "You're just lucky I'm helping you."

"I'm lucky!" said Jimmy. "You told me she was shut up in the bedroom. That's why I thought it was OK to open the back door."

"Well, anyway," Kit told him, "we'd better find her before dinner, or Auntie Coates is going to have a fit."

That stopped the argument. Auntie Coates was staying with the boys while their dad was up in Porterville, looking for work. She had a temper like a volcano and a tongue like a razor. Nobody wanted to make her mad.

Jimmy said, "Let's look down by the garbage cans."

"OK," Kit agreed. They clattered down the steps to the garbage cans by the side of the apartment building.

"Hah!" Kit exclaimed. "There she is!"

Jimmy looked and saw a fluffy white tail waving above a garbage can.

Kit walked up slowly. "Come here, Lady Fat Face," he said sweetly. He grabbed her from behind. "There! Now let go of that bone!" He tried to pull a chicken bone from the cat's mouth. She screeched.

"Let her keep it till you get her inside," Jimmy said.

"Good idea," Kit said. "Come on, sweetheart. No more slumming for you."

The boys snickered at the thought of their aunt's pampered darling rooting through the garbage.

Kit started upstairs with the cat. Jimmy was following when he saw the corner of a dollar bill under a can.

He bent and pulled it out. It wasn't a $1 bill. It was a $100 bill.

"Wow," Jimmy whispered.

Jimmy tilted the can to one side. Underneath was a paper bag. As he opened it, Jimmy held his breath. The bag was full of money. Jimmy began to count, his fingers shaking: 100 . . . 200 . . . 300 . . .

Kit called from the steps, "Come on, Jimmy! Open the door for me!"

Jimmy didn't hear him. He counted $1,500, and there was still a fat wad of bills left. His mind was racing. The things he could buy! The things he could do! Then he thought of his dad, out of work for two months. It had to go to Dad. It would save them all.

Suddenly, Kit was standing in front of him, his eyes on the money. Jimmy looked at his brother and stuffed the paper bag into his jacket.

Kit shook his head. "Better put that back where you found it, Jimmy," he told him in a low voice.

"I found it," Jimmy said. "We need it. Don't try to talk me out of it!" His voice rose.

"Shut *up*!" Kit hissed. "You want the whole block to hear you? Remember, somebody robbed Jadel's Liquors last night? The robbers were probably running away, and they left the money here. They're going to be back for it soon. Think about what they'll do to you when they find out you took it!"

"They're not going to find out," said Jimmy. "Look, Dad's got to have this!"

"That money would bring us nothing but trouble," Kit said. "You've got to leave it here or take it to the police."

Jimmy looked at his brother for a long moment. Then he made up his mind. He said . . .

Doing Time

Officers Lasker and Buell were patrolling Ward D of the county reformatory. Ward D was made up of six large rooms; each room held 12 boys. At the end of each room were large windows so that the officers could look in and see the two rows of bunk beds and the boys in the room. Pete Buell looked at his watch. It was 10:30 P.M. Their shift would be over in half an hour, and he was ready. They were passing Room 5 when Lasker grabbed Buell's arm. "Look at that . . . the kid sitting in the left bottom bunk."

"What?" asked Buell. "What was he doing?"

"It looked like he was stuffing something into that roll of toilet paper," Lasker replied. "Let's go."

Buell followed Lasker into the room. It was as if Lasker had eyes in the back of his head. Buell wondered if he'd ever be as quick as Lasker.

Buell followed Lasker up to the kid. The boy sat like a statue, his long hands dangling from his bony knees. Only his frightened eyes moved.

"Step out here," Lasker ordered, pointing to the space between the bunks.

The kid got up. He was almost as tall as Buell, but his face made him look about 11. He's a child, Buell thought. He should be home making paper airplanes.

Someone turned off the TV. The room became perfectly silent. Every boy was looking at the officers. Buell could feel the weight of all those staring eyes.

Lasker lifted the mattress. There was the roll of toilet paper. He turned it on one end. He poked his fingers into the paper and pulled out a small plastic bag. Lasker opened the bag, which contained about a spoonful of what looked like dirty white crumbs.

"Crack cocaine," Lasker said coldly. "You're in big, big trouble, kid."

The boy's voice was high, frantic. "It's not mine! It's not!" he cried.

Lasker turned to Buell. "I'm going to give you some practice. Report this guy while I look in on Room 6."

Lasker walked off. He looked big and powerful, even from the back.

Another boy walked up, a husky kid with quick black eyes. "Lasker stashed it," the boy said in a low voice.

Buell stared at him. "I'm telling the truth," the kid said. "I saw him put the toilet paper under that mattress this morning."

Buell looked up at the tall boy. The kid's eyes seemed to be begging him for help. Was he innocent or were these kids just good actors?

What about Lasker? He had gone straight for the bag as if he had X-ray eyes. But Lasker had been an officer for many years. Maybe that was why he knew where to look. Maybe Lasker was a cop who had gone rotten. The whole room was waiting. He could turn the boy in or go tell his supervisor about Lasker. At last he decided. He . . .

Sometimes, it seems like life is a series of turning points. What to say, how to act, what to believe—everyone wrestles with these issues every day, just like the people in this unit. You probably have a set of beliefs that guide your actions, but sometimes, things happen to make you question your beliefs. Deciding how to solve these problems helps us know who we are and what is important to us.

In this unit, people tackle a wide variety of problems, from deciding if taking steroids is a good idea to reporting suspected child abuse. When you answer the questions below, think about how you go about solving the turning points you face every day.

1. Why is Rick in "The Boy in the Mall" convinced that the little boy is in trouble?

2. What other explanation for the child's behavior in "The Boy in the Mall" could there be besides kidnapping?

3. In "Helping Hand," what choices does Raquel have besides accusing her mother of theft?

4. What can you tell about Raquel from what you learned in "Helping Hand"?

5. In "Team Spirit," what do you think Max's family's response would be if he decided to take the steroids? What would their response be if he quit the team?

6. Why do you think wrestling is so important to Max in "Team Spirit"? Why is it important to his family?

7. What do you think is the best reason for Bethany to take the job in "Managing"? What is the best reason for her to allow Lucy a chance at the job?

8. How do you think Joseph in "Managing" should choose a night manager?

9. Write at least two reasons that might explain why the parents have not come home or contacted Tina in "Parents, Please Come Home."

10. Think about the situation in "The Boy in the Mall." Is the situation in "Parents, Please Come Home" similar? Explain.

11. In "A Different Face," what do you think could explain Josie's stepfather's belief that people should only date others of their own culture?

12. Describe Josie in "A Different Face." Do these words describe someone who would be likely to defy her stepfather or not? Explain.

13. What do you think Cardell's brothers in "Big Money" would do if they were faced with this choice? Explain.

14. Write at least three ways "Big Money" could end.

15. Do you think Kit in "Treasure" is right to be as nervous as he is at the end? Explain.

16. In making his decision in "Doing Time," Pete has to think about the evidence. Why might he believe that Lasker is telling the truth? What shows he might be lying?

▮▮▮THINKING ABOUT THE ENDING

In this unit, characters have to make decisions based on their beliefs, on what they think is right, and on what their decisions might mean to others. Choose one story, and think about how you would end it.

As you think about your ending, consider the decision the character has to make. Is there another way to resolve the conflict? In your writing, describe how the character makes the decision and the effect that decision has on the other characters in the story.

*W*hite Water

When they told me about the trip, they said how exciting the rapids on the river would be. They said how the water would spray me in the face and that I would gasp and hang on. They didn't tell me I'd die. But when I looked down at the white water on the wild river, I was sure that was going to happen.

Back in Detroit, a summer in the mountains had sounded great. Here, watching the racing water slam into the sides of the canyon, all I wanted to do was to run back home to a boring summer. Not to mention the fact that I had somehow made an enemy, and we were spending the whole time fighting. With only eight kids on the trip, it wasn't like I could avoid her.

"Come on, Taneisha," Mr. Peters said in that fake hearty way of his. He put his hand on my shoulder. "Why don't you and Gloria try your hand at rafting together today? Maybe you'll patch up some of your differences."

"Sure, Mr. Peters," I said, in the same fake voice he used. He looked at me suspiciously.

Gloria and I got into the raft without looking at each other. So far, we'd been on the river two days and gone through some little rapids, where the water rushed down over rocks in the river. Those were scary enough. But when we looked at the white water down the river today, we could see that the rapids ahead were much bigger. Worse, down the river we could hear a sickening roar. That was Desolation, the worst rapids on the river. I was scared out of my mind, but I sure wasn't going to tell Gloria that.

"You want to row?" she asked.

"Sure," I said.

"Listen," she hissed, leaning forward, "I don't like you, and you don't like me. I don't owe you anything, and you don't owe me anything. Right?"

I nodded. We traded off doing the oaring all morning, not saying a word to each other.

She'd started it the very first day, during a hike, by making fun of my accent. I took a swing at her. Since then, things had only gotten worse.

I couldn't eat much lunch. Desolation was getting closer, and the howl of water smashing into the rocks below was constant. I was scared to death.

After lunch, I took my turn at the oars. I was going to have to row the rapids. In some ways, I was glad. At least I was in control. As we neared Desolation, my palms were so sweaty that they kept slipping off the oars. I was concentrating so hard that I didn't even see the storm blow in. Then the sky darkened. Rain began to pour down just as we entered the rapids. All I could see was white and black. Wind was whipping the boat, and rain was in my eyes.

"You idiot, we're going over sideways!" Gloria screamed, panic in her voice. "Pull over!"

"What do you think I'm trying to do?" I shouted back as the boat slipped over the edge and into a hole. Water thundered into the boat as it hit a rock and began to tip. Gloria was tossed out of the boat and into the water. At the same time, I saw a calm place on the side I could head for. At least I could save myself.

Then I heard Gloria scream as the river swept her past the next set of rocks. She'd said I didn't owe her anything. Should I make for the shore and safety?

Should I try to save Gloria? I didn't even know if I could steer the boat over there. To get her, I'd have to go over the worst rapids of all. I wasn't sure I could do it. Behind me, I saw another raft coming. Maybe they could pick her up. I hesitated, my oars in the air. Then I . . .

The Prisoner and the Proof

"You're taking the prisoner into town, Private," the sergeant ordered. "Here—don't lose these." The sergeant handed Jim a thick wad of papers. "These are statements by witnesses. Without them, we don't have a case."

Jim stuffed the papers into his pocket. "Yes, sir. . . . What's the prisoner accused of, sir?" he asked.

"He's a murderer, Private," the sergeant answered. "Dismissed!"

"Yes, sir!"

The prisoner was already in the jeep. "OK," Jim said. "Let's go."

The prisoner nodded, his eyes straight ahead.

The road led around the sharp curves of the mountain. The lights of the base soon disappeared as they drove into the freezing night. Jim could see nothing but a few yards of dirt road ahead of him. The prisoner sat silently. His hands, in handcuffs, lay quietly in his lap.

Jim slowed as the jeep came to a narrow drawbridge. The jeep started across, rumbling loudly over the thick wooden beams.

Suddenly, there was a terrible groaning and cracking noise. The jeep fell forward. The last thing Jim saw was the windshield in front of his eyes.

When he came to, his face was throbbing. He felt himself being jerked upward into the cold night air. He opened his eyes. The prisoner was pulling him out of the jeep.

"What . . . ?" he muttered.

"Come on," urged the prisoner. "Got to get out."

Jim looked around. One end of the drawbridge was still standing. The other end had fallen about 10 feet down the side of the cliff.

"The bridge must be hanging by a thread," the prisoner said. "I don't want to climb this cliff. Those rocks look loose. Let's go back up the bridge. Where's the key for the handcuffs?"

Jim's head hurt too much to think of another plan. He got the key out of his pants pocket and clicked open the prisoner's handcuffs. The prisoner let them fall into the icy river below.

They crawled slowly back up the bridge, holding on to the railing. The prisoner pulled Jim along. "Hurry!" he shouted, "Hurry! The bridge could fall any second!"

At last, they were near the end of the bridge. Jim's head was clearer now. He pushed ahead of the prisoner and stepped onto the road.

Suddenly, the crossbeams the prisoner was standing on gave way. With a yell, he threw himself forward. At that same instant, the jeep tumbled off the bridge and into the water. Its lights went out, and there was nothing to see but black night in every direction.

"Help!" The voice of the prisoner came from below.

"Where are you?" Jim yelled.

"I'm hanging onto one of the main beams," he called. "I don't know how long I can hold on." His voice was shaky, desperate.

Jim heard a slow creaking sound that sent a shiver up his back. He crawled to the edge of the road through darkness that was like the inside of a pocket. The crank for the drawbridge was very near, he knew. He could turn it, and what was left of the bridge would raise up, lifting the prisoner out of danger. If he could only see! Just a few moments of light would tell him where the lever was.

Then he thought of the matches in his pocket—and the folded papers. The papers could be twisted into a torch. However, those papers were the only proof that the prisoner was guilty of murder.

Jim thought frantically. This man might be a killer, he thought, but he saved my life. What should I do?

Jim made his decision. He . . .

*T*he Titanic Is Sinking!

John Gamble was dancing with the woman from the next cabin when they felt the jolt. "Oh, my!" she said brightly. "What was that?"

"Don't worry," John said, putting his arm around her more tightly. "This ship is unsinkable. Remember?"

"Oh, yes," she sighed. Others in the ballroom were less sure. While some people continued to dance, others were standing, talking. Their worried voices began to fill the ballroom. Soon, everyone had stopped dancing. John and his partner stood together.

"I don't understand this," John said, frowning. Then he realized that the engines had stopped. Slowly, the ship began to tilt.

Panicked, people in the ballroom rushed outside to the deck where others crowded along the railing. The woman John had been dancing with also ran outside.

"What's going on?" John asked one passing sailor, catching and shaking him.

"We've hit an iceberg, sir," the sailor said.

"So?" John asked.

The sailor looked at him with contempt. "So, sir, we are sinking," he said, shaking off John's hands.

"Sinking?" John said. His voice grew angrier and angrier. "Sinking! No. No! This ship cannot sink!"

There were nods of agreement on the deck among those who had heard John. Others, though, were desperately working their way to the lifeboats. The crew was trying to calm the crowd around the boats, filling them with children and women as fast as possible. Then the sailors released the boats over the side.

John realized that he was in a kind of shock. The water the *Titanic* was sailing through was as cold as ice. The ship had hit an iceberg, after all. He knew the ship was off the coast of Newfoundland now. What were the chances of any ships being near enough to rescue those who survived?

As John wandered the decks, he saw frantic people shoving and pushing to enter the lifeboats. It was clear that there were not enough lifeboats for all the passengers. How could this have happened? He felt a new surge of anger. The ship continued its tilt. Behind him, in the ballroom, he heard a crash as chairs and tables slid across the floor, smashing into the wall.

As the ship slid, John clung to a post and tried to think. The water was too cold to survive in. There were some lifeboats, but not enough. Should he try to shove aside one of the wild-eyed people at the railing and grab a spot in the boat? Perhaps he could jump in and hope to last long enough in the water to swim to a lifeboat. But would the people in the boats even let him on?

There was another crash as the ship tilted once more, dashing more dishes to the floor. Then again, John thought, I could stay on the ship. Perhaps there would be something to cling to on the ship. But what if the force of the water not only pulled the ship under, but also everyone foolish enough to stay aboard? John pushed his way to the railing and looked over at the black, freezing water below. He made his decision and . . .

The People Next Door

Stacy and Jana were at Jana's house, their books laid out on the kitchen table. There was a big math test tomorrow. They'd been studying for about a half-hour when Stacy groaned and laid her head down on her math book. "I hate this," she said. "It's so hard. Let's take a break and watch TV." The TV was on in the bedroom. Stacy could hear Jana's younger brother and sister laughing at some show they were watching.

Jana shook her head. "Better not," she said. "If we start watching TV, we'll never get through these chapters."

She bent back over her book. Stacy knew that she wouldn't be able to talk her into watching TV for at least an hour. Jana wasn't terribly smart, but she worked hard. Jana always said, I don't want to be a grocery clerk when I get out of school. Jana's mom was a grocery clerk, and she complained about her job constantly.

Stacy didn't want to end up a grocery-store clerk, either. But today she just couldn't concentrate. She got up from the table and wandered over to the window.

As she looked out, a car drove up to the neighbors' house—and parked in the driveway. Two men got out and walked quickly to the door. As they stood in front of the door, the older man turned to the younger one and said something. The younger man pulled a thick wad of money from his pants pocket and gave it to the older man, who put it in his jacket.

Stacy moved quickly away from the window. "Jana!" she said. "I just saw some guys going into your neighbors house—with a whole lot of money!"

"Which neighbors?" Jana asked, frowning.

Stacy had a feeling Jana knew exactly who she meant. "Those two guys next door," she replied. "Every time I've been here since they moved in, they've had people coming over, nonstop."

"So?" Jana asked.

"I think they're drug dealers," Stacy explained. She gave her friend a long look. "You think they're drug dealers, too, don't you?"

"I think they might be," Jana admitted.

"So let's call the police," Stacy said. "Where's your phone book?"

"Stacy!" Jana exclaimed. "We don't have any proof!"

"I'm going to report suspicious activity," said Stacy.

Jana cried, "Don't! That's crazy! They could kill us!" Jana's eyes were wide with fear. Stacy stared at her, amazed. She couldn't remember Jana ever being afraid.

Stacy said, "Jana, look at how scared you are. You can't live like this. Nobody can. You've got to stand up for yourself."

"Yeah, stand up and get shot," Jana said.

"I think we should call the police," Stacy replied. "But I won't do it if you don't want to."

Jana bit her lip and thought. "Stacy," she said slowly, "I think we should . . .

The Test of Fire

José woke up knowing that something was wrong. Then he smelled the smoke. The apartment was black and silent. Everyone else was asleep. The smell became stronger. It was a fire. José sat upright in his bed, his heart tight in his chest. His greatest fear was coming true. He and his family would all be trapped in this fire. They would all die.

"Mom?" he called. "Felicia? María?" There was no answer. José took a sharp breath to try to calm himself. They were still sleeping. He had to wake them up. José swung his feet to the ground. The floor was hot.

Suddenly, there was noise. Sirens began to whine in the distance. José heard the sound of breaking glass. Then he heard the panicked voice of his sister. "Mommy! Mommy!" Felicia was sobbing.

"José! José! Where are you? I can't see anything! There's a fire! Fire!" María was shouting.

"Girls? José?" That was his mother. If José had always been frightened of fire, his mother's fear was worse. She remembered the fire in the apartment building when he was a baby. Many of their friends hadn't made it out alive. He could imagine his mother paralyzed inside the room, waiting to die with his sisters.

Before he spoke, José steadied himself so that his voice would sound as calm as possible. "There's a fire. It's going to be all right," he yelled over the noise. "I'm coming to find you."

The lights suddenly went out. There was screaming everywhere now. José held a shirt to his face and groped his way to the door. The doorknob was hot. He used the end of his T-shirt to open it and then pulled the shirt across his mouth to shield his lungs from the smoke.

Choking smoke rolled into the room. José crouched down and fought his way through the blackness, his eyes stinging. Each breath burned.

"María, Felicia, Momma," he said through the shirt as he reached their room, "I'm here. It'll be all right. Get down and put something over your mouths. I'm opening the door now. Grab me."

Somehow, through the screaming, the crying, and the terrible black smoke, José got the three of them out the door of the apartment and down the three stories to the street. They stumbled to the ground holding each other and crying.

"My blankie," María was crying. José's mother was wide-eyed. Felicia was on her lap. Momma was patting Felicia's hair, rocking back and forth, not saying a word. The flames were spreading, orange sheets blasting from the windows. Then, during a time when the sirens were silent and there was only the roar of the fire, José heard a thin, terrified voice. It was their neighbor, Mrs. Peterson. "Someone help me!" she screamed.

The fire was spreading. He could still hear the sirens, but there were no firetrucks yet. If someone was going to save Mrs. Peterson, it would have to be José. He thought about his terror of fire. There was a chance he would not make it out alive if he went in after her. But if he didn't, she would die. Should he die to save one old woman? José put his head in his hands. Maybe there was another answer. A blanket. Could he get her to jump into a blanket? Maybe he could talk her down. But if he went to look for a blanket, it could be too late. As he was thinking, he could hear crashes in the building as the fire raged. Fighting down a sense of panic, José tried to think calmly. He looked into the fire's black smoke and made his decision. Then he . . .

*T*he Danger Outside

Chris got up from the couch where he and Dave were watching TV. "Want a soda?" he asked.

"Sure," Dave answered.

The kitchen was even hotter than the living room. Chris put lots of ice in the glasses. He sighed. It was a perfect Saturday to go swimming. He and Dave could be on their bikes and at the pool in ten minutes. But Chris was stuck baby-sitting the twins. His mom was working Saturdays lately. Chris hated it.

He opened the screen door and peeked out at the shady part of the lawn where the twins were playing. Lisa was laying her doll on an old cloth napkin, and Kirsten was going through a box of play dishes.

In spite of the heat, all the neighbors seemed to be outside. He could hear the Raymond boys arguing next door and more kids running around the Talbott's deck. He shut the door quietly. If the twins saw him, they'd beg him to play.

He walked back through the kitchen. Then he heard the sound of the garbage-can lid clattering to the ground. He looked out the window to the side yard. A large brown dog was standing on its hind legs, looking into the garbage can.

"Hey!" Chris yelled. He walked over to the window.

The dog looked up and snarled. Suddenly, it jumped. Before he knew what he was doing, Chris slammed down the window. For an instant, the huge mouth was very close—the yellow-white teeth were inches from his face. Then the dog was back on the ground, its eyes fixed on Chris. A cold, prickly feeling spread over Chris's scalp.

The dog flipped a take-out pizza box out of the can and ripped it open with a single jerk of its jaws.

"Dave . . ." Chris's voice was low and shaky.

Dave hurried into the kitchen. "What?" Then he saw the dog. "Look at the shoulders on him!" he exclaimed. "That's a pit bull."

"It just jumped at me," Chris said. "If I hadn't closed the window in time . . ."

Dave said, "We'd better call 911."

"That'll take too long," Chris said. "The twins are playing right around the corner!" A chill went through him when he thought of the twins. All the dog had to do was walk from the side yard to the backyard where Kirsten and Lisa were. The girls would run right up to the pit bull. They thought every dog was their best friend.

Dave said, "Well, think of something else, then— quick!"

Chris knew what he had to do. He . . .

Danger can arise anywhere. Sometimes, it jumps out at us in strange territory, such as on a ship. At other times, danger is as close as the neighbor's yard. Many of us have never had to face a real crisis, where our actions may make the difference between life and death for ourselves or someone else. But sometimes, people become involved in situations that require deciding who lives— and who dies.

In this unit, you have a chance to think about how you might react and others might react in dangerous situations. Some involve choosing whether to risk one's own life to save someone else. Others involve just trying to save oneself. Think about what your reaction might be and what the character's might be, as you answer the questions below.

1. What can you tell about Taneisha from what you have read in "White Water"?

2. At the end of "White Water," do you think Gloria would still agree that Taneisha doesn't owe her anything? Explain.

3. How could you save the prisoner's life in "The Prisoner and the Proof" and not have to burn the papers?

4. How do the prisoner's and Jim's roles change as the story in "The Prisoner and the Proof" unfolds? Give examples from the story.

5. Why does John Gamble not understand what is happening on the *Titanic*?

6. List three possible actions John might take at the end of "The *Titanic* Is Sinking!"

7. Do you think Jana is right to be afraid of her neighbors in "The People Next Door"?

8. What should Stacy consider as she makes her decision about what to do in "The People Next Door"?

9. Why is José so afraid of fire? How does his fear affect his decision at the end of "The Test of Fire"?

10. List what you know about José in "The Test of Fire." What decision do you think he will make?

11. List two possible ways that Chris could save the twins in "The Danger Outside."

12. Do you think the boys are right to be as frightened as they are of the dog in "The Danger Outside"? Explain.

IIIIII THINKING ABOUT THE ENDING

In this unit, danger is the theme. The characters face dangers from rivers, fires, vicious dogs—even from neighbors. Solving these problems and getting out alive is their goal. Choose a story that you would like to finish. As you think about an ending, be creative. Is there another way to solve the crisis that the main character hasn't yet considered?

Write an ending for the story you choose. The ending doesn't have to be a happy one. It only has to make sense and be true to the rest of the story. Before you decide on an ending, make sure that the solution is one the character in the story would have found. Then show how the decision effects the other characters in the story.

'Tis the Gift to Be Simple

"Boy! What are you doing alone? Come inside!" Juan's mother snapped. "Don't embarrass me. It's Christmas!"

Juan was startled. He turned and looked up at his mother. She was standing in the open doorway. He could smell the spicy food and the sweat from the house.

Juan had been standing out on the porch alone. It was cold, but he didn't mind being outside. He didn't like this house. It was crowded, noisy, and smelly.

Juan had never met his mom's family. She had never mentioned them. The only place that was home to him was his mom and dad's apartment back in Ohio.

After Juan's dad left them, Mom packed up everything. They moved here to New Jersey, to this tiny old house.

"This was my home when I was little like you," his mom said. "Now it's our home."

That home was filled with strangers called relatives.

Juan took one last breath of fresh air and went back inside. He looked around the living room. The adults sat on the sofa and chairs. One woman had a baby. They were playing with it.

The kids were a little older than Juan. They were playing with the toys they had been given for Christmas.

Juan wished he had toys to play with, too, but he didn't get any presents for Christmas.

"Maybe next year," Juan's mother had told him.

Juan looked for her. She was with the other adults playing with the baby. He had never seen her like this. She was laughing and speaking in Spanish to her brothers and sisters.

Juan's mother looked up from the baby. She made an angry face at him. It said, Behave!

Mom had been trying to get him to play with his cousins all day. She didn't understand that they didn't want to play with him. They were more interested in their toys. He stood quietly against the wall. He wanted to go back to his old home.

His grandmother came out of the kitchen into the living room. She was the only person he knew, aside from his mother. All the kids ran up to her, showing her their toys. Juan watched how she bent down to kiss the girls and hug the boys.

Juan's grandmother looked at him standing alone. "Merry Christmas," she said in English. She handed him a ten-dollar bill from her pocket.

This embarrassed Juan. Everyone was looking at him.

"Say 'thank you'!" his mom yelled.

"Thank you," Juan said shyly. He had never had this much money. He wondered what he would do with it.

"Stick 'em up!" someone said in Spanish.

Juan looked up. One of the boys was pointing a toy gun at his face. Should he play along?

"Give me your money!" the boy said in Spanish. He motioned for Juan to hand the money to him.

Juan looked at his mom.

"Give him your money," she said. All the adults were laughing.

Is he serious? Juan wondered. Why do I have to give it to him?

He looked at his mother again. She glared at him with that face that said, Behave!

Juan looked sadly at his present and then at the boy with the gun. He . . .

Robbery in Progress

"Have you heard anything from that brother of yours?" Gerry asked, stuffing his sausage sandwich in his mouth.

"No," Ramón said, watching his partner lick sauce from his fingers. "Nobody's heard from him in months."

"It makes you wonder," Gerry said, yawning and stretching in the patrol car. "I mean, look at the two of you. Brothers. What makes the difference? Here you are, a model cop, and there he is. Scum."

"He's my older brother," Ramón said, trying to keep the anger out of his voice. "I love him. Stay out of it."

"Back off, pal. Okay? He's been in and out of jail for drugs and petty burglary since I've known you. You made it; he didn't. I just wonder why."

Ramón sighed and ran his hand over his head. "Let's just skip it, all right?"

The dispatcher had been dribbling out the usual stream of words on the police radio. Suddenly, the voice became urgent.

"Robbery in progress, First National Bank, 3173 Clayton." That was five blocks from where they were. Gerry crumpled up the paper from his sandwich.

"Let's go," he said.

Ramón flipped on the siren and put his foot on the gas. The car took off. In 15 seconds, Ramón skidded the car to a halt, and they were out of the car, guns drawn.

Ramón heard a gunshot and tensed. Three figures in black ski masks ran full speed from the bank, heading in different directions. "I'll take him," Ramón shouted, pointing at one man. Gerry nodded and motioned with his gun toward a second figure.

Ramón ran quickly and then put on a burst of speed, his breath burning in his chest. He was closing in when the robber turned to fire. As he turned, he tripped. The bullet went wild. Ramón ducked, took a flying leap, and landed on the robber's back.

"Drop it. Hands up," Ramón demanded. The gun clattered to the ground. Ramón cuffed the robber's hands, turned him over, pulled off the ski mask—and found himself looking into the eyes of his brother.

"Luís!"

"Hey, Ramón. How're you doing?" Luís asked, with his crooked smile. When they were young, Luís could get his younger brother to do anything when he flashed that smile.

"Great. Just great," Ramón said angrily. "Luís, what were you thinking? This isn't small-time stuff. This is serious. This is bank robbery. You'll be in jail for years."

"Doesn't have to be," Luís said. "You never saw me. I'm your brother. Remember what that means? Or is that blue uniform more important than family?"

Ramón stared at him.

"Listen," Luís said rapidly, "all you've got to do is let me up. No one has to know. You do this, and I promise I'll go straight. I promise. You can be my probation officer. Give me another chance, Ramón. If you arrest me now, it's all over. I'm in jail for good. Think of Mom. You want her to go through this? Come on, bro, let me go!"

Ramón looked at Luís. Then he . . .

 **B**read

Mark heard his mom call him over the noise of the TV. He clicked it off and walked to her room. She lay on the bed, a towel over her head, still in her work clothes.

"Do we have bread?" she asked.

"No," Mark answered. "I used it for today's lunch."

"Well, go and buy more then."

It was late, but Mark didn't mind going down the block to the supermarket. He did it all the time to get bread, and sometimes peanut butter. That's all he and his mother could afford. He still liked to go, though, just to hang out. The video games didn't interest him. He never had the extra money or the desire to play them. He liked to walk up and down the aisles and look at all the cupcakes and snacks.

"Get peanut butter, too," said his mom.

"Yuck," said Mark quietly to himself.

Mark waited as his mom rolled over to the side of her bed. He watched her reach down and open her purse.

"Here's five dollars," she said.

Mark took the money without looking at it. He stuffed it into his pocket and then headed for the door.

"Make sure to get day-old bread," she called.

They always got day-old bread. It was cheaper.

Mark put on a sweatshirt. He was about to leave the apartment when he stopped.

"Mom?"

"Yes?"

"Is it OK if I get something else?"

His mom sat up. "What?"

Mark knew what she would say, but he tried anyway. "Can I get something else besides peanut butter and bread?"

"What do you mean by something else?"

This was the way it always went. He kept trying.

"The other kids in school get snacks, like cupcakes."

"You know we can't afford it . . ." she began.

Yes, he knew. Mark watched as his mother lay back down. He wanted to tell her how he hated having peanut butter every day. He wanted to tell her about the snacks the other moms packed. He wanted to tell her how he hated finishing lunch and watching all the other kids crinkle the colorful packages and bite into their desserts. He wanted to tell her lots of things. But he didn't.

"We're lucky to have peanut butter," his mom said "Someday, I'll buy you everything you want. But for now, it has to be peanut butter."

Mark turned and walked out of the apartment. He thought about getting one thing for himself. Something small, cheap, and sweet. He had tried one of those snacks once. His friend had let him have a bite. That bite had only made him want more. All he knew was that he wanted something else besides a peanut butter sandwich. He wanted anything that would keep the other kids from feeling sorry for him. He hated that the most.

Just once he'd like to go up to the checker at the supermarket with more than a loaf of old bread and a jar of peanut butter. One day, he would go to the regular lane, not the express lane. He wanted to see the surprised look on the checker's face when he bought the whole store.

"Keep the change!" he'd say laughingly.

Mark made his way to the store. Before he went in, he checked to see if the money was still in his pocket. He pulled it out and looked at it.

His mother had made a mistake. In his hand was a ten-dollar bill, not a five. Mark stared at the money for a long time. Then he . . .

Many Happy Returns

"No, and that's final. Understand?"

Marcy's mother bit off her words. Marcy sighed and pressed her lips together to stop the tears.

"Mom, I don't ask for much," she said, her voice shaking. "But if I don't have the money, I can't compete in the gymnastics meet. It's as simple as that."

Marcy's mother sighed and put an arm around her. "Oh, honey, I'm so sorry. You know that. But we just don't have it. I've been trying to find a job that pays more."

Now her mother was starting to get tears in her eyes. "Mom, this is getting ridiculous," Marcy sobbed, and then laughed. "We're both sitting here crying."

"Everything they say about being a single mother is true," Marcy's mother said, wiping her eyes. "It's lonely, it's hard, and it's making do. What they never talk about, though, is how your daughter can make you forget about the pain." She hugged Marcy. "Let me see if I can talk to Mrs. Peterson. She's always said she'd pay anything for one of my lemon pies. You could help."

"I'll walk to Florida and get the lemons," Marcy said.

Her mother laughed and walked over to answer the knock at the door.

"Carl!" her mother said in a voice that Marcy had never heard before. She sounded shocked, upset. Could this Carl be Marcy's father? The one who had walked out when Marcy was only 3? Marcy got up and looked at the thin, tall man at the door smiling an uncertain smile.

"Is that my Marcy?" he asked.

Marcy was suddenly filled with feelings she didn't know she had. "Your Marcy? Your Marcy?" she asked angrily. "Who are you kidding? You left us. Remember?"

"Now, Marcy, calm down," her mother said. Then she turned to the man. "What are you doing here? It's late for a family reunion, isn't it?"

"Listen to me for a minute, just a minute," the man at the door pleaded. "You think this is easy, coming back, facing you? It isn't. But I had to. I can't say I was right to leave, but how can you tell me I can't come back and help? Look at this place! You could use some help."

"You've got no call to laugh at the way we live," Marcy's mother said. "I work hard. I stayed put and took care of our daughter. You? We don't know you."

"Marcy," he said, turning to his daughter, "I know you haven't forgiven me. But can't you give me a chance?"

"You don't deserve her," Marcy's mother said. "I don't want you making nice with her. I don't want you coming in here being the big, generous daddy. Get out."

"Let me help you," Marcy's father said. "I make a good living now. All I want to do is help."

"We don't need your money," Marcy's mother said. "Do we, Marcy?"

"Let's let Marcy decide that," her father said. "Let me try to make it up to you, Marcy. Let me start to support you like I should have all along. I'm not asking for much. I just want to get to know you. What do you say, Marcy?"

"Well," said Marcy . . .

*T*he Hat

Bobby dropped to his hands and knees and peered under the bed. He was in a hurry, so if his favorite hat wasn't under there, he'd have to go without it. He had to meet Jessie in a half-hour, and she adored that hat. If he could find it, she might adore him, too.

Bobby stood up and brushed himself off. "Sam!" he hollered. "Did you take my hat again, Sam?"

"Yeah," his brother answered. "I need it, but I promise I'll give it back to you tomorrow."

When Bobby heard the front door slam, he thought about chasing his brother, but he knew he'd never catch him. His brother was too fast. His speed was just one of the things he had learned in jail.

Jessie was late. Bobby shuffled around on the corner for an hour, waiting for her.

Just then, Jessie turned the corner. "Let's get something to eat," she said. "I'm starving."

They went to the diner on the corner and sat in the last booth. He wanted to hold her hand, but he knew that she wouldn't let him yet. He had to be funny and interesting and clever first.

"I couldn't find my favorite hat," he said. "I wanted to give it to you." He hadn't even thought of giving it to her until that moment, but it was a good idea.

Two policemen came in the door. They stopped at their booth and glared down at Bobby.

One of the cops held up the hat and asked, "Does this belong to you?"

Bobby shrugged and muttered, "Yeah, why?"

"We found it in a stolen car, and somebody said he'd seen you wearing it."

Bobby hesitated. "It's just a baseball cap," he responded. "Anybody could have a hat like that."

"Notice the words *Chain Reaction* on the hat, Bobby?" the other cop added. "Now, how many people do you think have those words written on their cap?"

"Chain Reaction is a band," Bobby said. "I'm sure they made more than one hat."

"You'll have to come with us," the cop said.

"Tell him," Jessie whispered, leaning closer.

Bobby shook his head at her. What was he supposed to tell the cop? Should he explain that his brother had borrowed his hat? If he did, his brother would probably go to jail. Should he tell the cop that his brother had taken care of him all his life? Should he explain that when his brother went to prison for armed robbery, Bobby had been left all alone?

Jessie was frowning at him with sad, curious eyes.

"How about the hat?" Bobby asked the cop.

He wanted to give the hat to Jessie before he went wherever he was going. He knew if he took the rap for his brother, they wouldn't be too hard on him. After all, it would be only his first offense.

"It's evidence," the cop said.

Jessie was still waiting for him to speak out and explain his situation. "Tell him," she pleaded.

"I don't know what to say," Bobby whispered.

"Let's go, Bobby," the cop said impatiently.

Bobby stood up, faced both cops, and said . . .

Families are the people we live with, the people we love, and, sometimes, the people we wish would leave us alone. Families shape us in many ways. They help explain who we are and why we think the way we do. Whether we like it or not, our ties to our families last forever.

The stories in this unit explore different family situations. Use what you've learned about families through your own experience and the experience of others to help you answer the questions that follow.

1. In "'Tis the Gift to Be Simple," why is Juan's mother angry with him?

2. What do you think Juan could do to try to fit in at the party in " 'Tis the Gift to Be Simple"? How could his mother help him?

3. Why do you think Ramón might let his brother go in "Robbery in Progress"? Why might he arrest him?

4. Do you think Luís's pleas are working with Ramón in "Robbery in Progress"? How can you tell?

5. What do you think the consequences would be if Mark bought himself a treat at the end of "Bread"?

6. Why do you think Mark longs for a snack in "Bread"?

7. Describe the relationship Marcy and her mother have in "Many Happy Returns."

8. In "Many Happy Returns," why do you think Carl has decided to come back?

9. At the end of "The Hat," describe how you think Bobby is feeling about his brother.

10. What can you tell about the relationship between the brothers in "The Hat"?

11. Compare the relationships between the brothers in "Robbery in Progress" and "The Hat." How are they similar? How are they different?

In the stories in this unit, the main characters have to make decisions about their families or about a family member. How far should loyalty to a family member go? How much does someone owe his or her family? Think about one of the stories in this unit that interested you. How do the family members act and feel toward one another? What decision does the character have to make about his or her family?

Write an ending to the story in which you take all these questions into consideration. Write not only what the main character decides, but how he or she comes to a decision. Include what the results of the decision are for all of the members of the character's family.

In the Colony of Saurnia

Oct. 13

I'll say this about Saurnia. They make it easy for you. I mean, there's something comforting about knowing exactly what I'm going to be doing in 5 years or next year or 20 years from now. I will be a mechanic. I will be working on the engines of the new Moor rocket systems. They take all the worry out of deciding what to do.

June 4

I just read that paragraph I wrote last October. I realize that, even then, I was trying to convince myself that I really wanted to be a mechanic. I should want to do it. It's a good job. It's one of the most important jobs on the planet. It's well paid. More important, it's what I'm supposed to do. I was born to do it. That's what they told me, anyway. They put mechanic's genes in me before I was born.

Then why am I so miserable? I'll tell you why. I want to be an artist. I want to paint pictures that people love to look at. If I have to be a mechanic, I'll be miserable my whole life. In a way, I'm mad at the doctors. If they had wanted to program me to be a mechanic, they should have done a better job. I should want to do it, but I don't.

All my friends know what they are going to be, and every one of them is happy. Why can't I be, too?

Yesterday, my friend Jori told me to stop talking about it. "You're going to be a mechanic," she said. "Get used to it. You're good at it. You'll make a good living. Anyway, you don't have a choice and you know it. For this colony to survive, we all have to do what we're supposed to. What if everyone wanted to be an artist? We'd starve. So keep quiet about it. You don't have any choice."

But I can't stop thinking about it. Sometimes, I think I'll die of boredom if I become a mechanic. Doesn't every society need artists, too? Why do we have to only have art from other planets? Why can't we make our own?

Last week, I found out about a group of people who live outside the colony. They're rebels. Like me, they don't want to do what they were programmed for.

I know what Jori would say. She would talk about how being what you want to be may be great in other places, but here it's a matter of life and death. She'd talk about how this colony needs everyone doing his or her job or the society will fall apart. She'd talk about how we all depend on one another.

The problem is that I don't know if I believe that anymore. So what if one person or a group of people decides to do something different? Should I spend my whole life doing something I can't stand? I'd almost rather have the colony fall apart. Maybe a place that has to program everyone to do jobs doesn't deserve to exist.

Maybe I've been too hasty. Maybe I can be an artist in my spare time. If I don't become a mechanic, maybe Saurnia will be in trouble. I don't want that to happen.

The rebels have asked me if I want to join them. They want an answer by tomorrow. I told them I'd think about it tonight and give them an answer. The problem is that I really don't know what to tell them. No, that's not true. I know what I'll say. I'll tell them . . .

Kavlon V

"EE-EE-EE! EE-EE-EE!" the ear-splitting alarm rang through the mine shaft. The foreman came running up to Captain Mark Traven.

"What's going on?" the foreman shouted.

"Meteor shower!" Traven yelled.

The men looked at one another. They had known the meteor shower was coming. They should have started back to Earth yesterday. But the miners had struck a rich vein of valuable minerals. Traven and the foreman decided to stay one more day and the men had agreed. There was a lot of money to be made on Kavlon V.

"Make a run for the ship," Traven screamed. "I'll make sure everyone gets out of here."

The men began to hurry out of the mine, dusty and sweating in their heavy mining suits. Most were carrying bags of mineral-rich dirt and rock. Traven ticked off their names in his head as they went by: Weston, Dean, Khorram, Pruitt . . .

"Drop the drill! Leave it!" Traven yelled to Roberts. Roberts dropped the drill and ran.

More men passed: Davis, Merrill, Chin, Stern . . .

"EE-EE-EE!" The alarm was making Traven's head throb. He began to trot toward the entrance to the mine shaft. One more man, Weston, ran past. Good, Traven thought. Everyone's out. He hurried past the heavy gate at the entrance to the mine shaft, not bothering to lock it. Every second counted now.

Ahead, through the whirling orange dust, he could see the rusty nose of the ship.

Suddenly, he realized he hadn't seen Sellon come out. He turned around and saw the meteor—a huge gray rock zooming down from the sky like a runaway train. He screamed and began to run.

It hit the entrance of the mine shaft with a crash that shook the ground. A great cloud of orange dust rose up.

Traven ran to the entrance of the mine shaft. The thick metal poles at the gate had bent like straws. The entrance was sealed up by rocks and dirt.

"Sellon!" Traven screamed. "Sellon!"

"I'm inside!" Sellon's voice came faintly through the rocks and dirt.

Traven thought quickly. It would take an hour, at least, to dig Sellon out. He thought of what the meteor storm might do to the ship and the men in an hour.

Sellon's voice came again from inside his rocky prison. "Leave me! You can't risk everyone's lives just for me!"

Traven thought about Sellon's quiet laugh and the box of pretty rocks he had been saving for his three daughters. Could he put them all at risk to save one man? As he thought, he found the answer to his question. Then he . . .

*H*ow Do You Say "Friend"?

The siren sounded again. The natives of Stratus were launching another attack. Sam sighed. Not again, he thought. It's the third time this week. People were hurrying, heads down, toward shelters. They look like scared ants, Sam thought. I'm not going. I'm staying right here. I can't live my life running for shelter every second.

Somehow, that thought made Sam feel more free than he had in months. Grinning, he ran toward a city park that looked just like the ones back on Earth—if you could get over the fact that the grass was painted and the trees were inky black. Sam hid under one of the trees.

Suddenly, he heard a rustling in the bushes. He froze. Maybe I'm not so brave after all, he thought, as his heart pounded. If a Stratan caught him, he was as good as dead.

Through the dense black leaves, Sam could make out a jagged mane of hair. It was a Stratan. Except for the mane, they looked human. All the bulletins, though, talked about how fierce Stratans were. Stratans hated humans. Their only goal was to get them to leave the planet and return to Earth. However, because the shuttles carrying the colonists had all been destroyed when they reached the planet's surface, that wasn't likely. The colonists were on Stratus to stay—unless, of course, the natives killed them.

Sam held his breath. Then he saw that the Stratan was looking right at him. I'm dead, Sam thought. For a long moment, the two beings stared at one another. Then the Stratan did something completely unexpected. He spoke.

"Human," the Stratan said, reaching out his hand.

Sam was amazed. Few Stratans had learned English.

"Hello," Sam said timidly. He didn't offer his hand—no one knew what diseases Stratans might be carrying.

"Human," the Stratan repeated. "I want to be friends."

Friends? Sam was shocked. This was unheard of. Stratans and humans had never been able to hold a conversation without someone firing a laser.

"Our leaders must talk," the Stratan said. "Too much death."

"You got that right," Sam muttered. Then he said, loud enough for the Stratan to hear, "Why do you kill us?"

The Stratan shook his head. "We do not know you. You come here and take everything. Of course we kill. But that must change. Come with me. Our leaders must talk."

"I'm no one!" Sam protested. "I have no power! I'm a young person. No one will listen to me. If your people see me, they will kill me. If my people see me, they will kill us both. You should talk to someone with power."

"No," the Stratan said. "Now is our chance for peace. Now the leaders must meet. You can help bring them."

"But it might not even work. I might be killed just getting there," Sam pleaded. "What good will that do?"

"Now," the Stratan said, holding out his hand.

Sam looked at him. Who knew what this Stratan was really thinking? Sam had never heard of a Stratan being friendly or wanting peace. It could be a trap. The Stratans could be looking for a hostage. But what if he was sincere?

"Are you coming?" the Stratan asked.

Sam looked at him for a long moment and . . .

The only thing that can limit what a science-fiction writer writes is the distance his or her imagination can travel. In these stories, people face unearthly problems. They are deciding whether to risk the lives of several people to save one man, to trust an alien, and to defy a world government.

As you answer the questions below, use your knowledge of the way people behave on Earth to think about how they might behave on another world. Remember that even though the situations they face are out of this world, they are still Earthlings making the decisions. They can, however, use the tools or ideas that you invent to help them.

1. Describe how the writer's mind seems to change as he writes in the diary in "In the Colony of Saurnia." Why do you think he changes?

2. In "In the Colony of Saurnia," what do you think the rebels hope to gain?

3. In "Kavlon V," do you think Traven has the right to put the entire crew in danger to try to save one person? Explain.

4. Because this is science fiction, stretch your imagination and come up with an unexpected solution to Traven's problem in "Kavlon V."

5. Why should Sam believe the Stratan in "How Do You Say 'Friend' "? What reasons does Sam have for mistrusting him?

6. How do you think Sam could convince his leaders to meet with the Stratans?

In this unit, the characters have to use their intelligence and their feelings to find ways to deal with strange, new situations. Choose one of the stories. How does the main character behave? Is the situation different from one he or she might encounter on Earth?

Based on what you know about the main character, how would that person choose to solve the problem? Remember that this is science fiction. Make the main character's behavior realistic, but remember that just about anything goes!